D0341927

MUSIC FOR SIGHT SINGING

3rd edition

MUSIC FOR SIGHT SINGING

ROBERT W. OTTMAN
North Texas State University

PRENTICE-HALL, ENGLEWOOD CLIFFS, N.J. 07632

Library of Congress Cataloging-in-Publication Data
Ottman, Robert W.
Music for sight singing.

1. Sight-singing. I. Title.
MT870.O86 1986 784.9'4 85-25616
ISBN 0-13-607532-0 (pbk.)

Editorial/production supervision and
interior design: Marina Harrison
Cover design: Karen Stephens
Manufacturing buyer: Ray Keating
Page layout: Steve Frim

Printed in the United States of America

10 9 8 7 6 5 4 3 2

ISBN 0-13-607532-0 01

Prentice-Hall International (UK) Limited, *London*
Prentice-Hall of Australia Pty. Limited, *Sydney*
Prentice-Hall of Canada Inc., *Toronto*
Prentice-Hall Hispanoamericana, S.A., *Mexico*
Prentice-Hall of India Private Limied, *New Delhi*
Prentice-Hall of Japan, Inc., *Tokyo*
Prentice-Hall of Southeast Asia Pte. Ltd., *Singapore*
Editora Prentice-Hall do Brasil, Ltda., *Rio de Janeiro*
Whitehall Books Limited, *Wellington, New Zealand*

CONTENTS

(R) *indicates Rhythmic Reading exercises*

PREFACE

To become successful in sight singing, one must have at his or her disposal a considerable amount of singable and musical material. This material should be graded so that the student will be able to study one problem, rhythmic or melodic, at a time and to progress steadily from the easiest material to the most complex. The music and examples in this collection, compiled with both these aims in mind, have been drawn from the literature of composed music and from a wide range of the world's folk music.

Skill in sight singing is dependent upon the ability to perform both rhythmic and melodic patterns. For this reason, the melodies in this volume are graded according to both rhythmic and melodic difficulty. Each chapter introduces a new problem in relation to one or the other factor, but not to both simultaneously. Because the material is so minutely graded, the order of chapters or sections within chapters may easily be shifted to suit various teaching procedures.

Although this third edition retains the concepts and the format of previous editions, several new features are designed to make the text pedagogically more effective.

Organization. The text as a whole is divided into four parts, each corresponding to one semester of the usual four-semester theory sequence. Though the use of the materials in the order presented will produce successful results, the organization allows the student to pursue the study of some particular rhythmic or melodic problem, after its initial presentation, by skipping to those sections of a following chapter presenting the problem on the next higher level.

Rhythm. In those chapters presenting a new problem in rhythm, the melodies are preceded by rhythmic exercises illustrating that problem, both as single line drills and as rhythmic duets.

Scale-line melodies. To simplify the students' earliest efforts in sight singing, the first chapter includes melodies made up exclusively of scale-wise passages. These (and these alone in this text) have been written specifically for sight singing purposes, as such melodies are rare in music literature.

Two-part examples. In addition to the large number of canons, both new and retained from earlier editions, most chapters now contain a separate section of duets. These include folk songs with a second part added by the author, and duets from sources in music literature.

Other traditional materials. New sections include the use of secondary dominant harmony and other altered chords, such as the Neapolitan sixth chord, as implied in melodic lines. In the book as a whole, a large proportion of the melodies will be familiar to users of previous editions, while many new melodies and duets chosen for their musical and pedagogical qualities have been added.

Twentieth century melody. A new chapter is devoted to this important study. It includes drills in contemporary uses of rhythm and pitch, and a selection of melodies representative of twentieth century compositional practices.

ACKNOWLEDGMENTS

The author expresses his appreciation to the following individuals and publishers for the use of melodies from their publications. Acknowledgements not listed here will be found immediately following the melodies concerned.

Victor Bator, trustee of the Bartók estate: melodies 103, 724, 830, and 962 from *Hungarian Folk Music* by Bela Bartók, published by Oxford University Press, Inc., New York, N.Y.

Mary O. Eddy, author of *Ballads and Songs from Ohio,* published by J. J. Augustin, Locust Valley, N.Y.: melodies 106, 446, and 537.

American Folklore Society, Philadephia, Pa.: melodies 101, 247, 824, 842, and 843 from the *Journal of American Folklore:* melodies 266, 481, 570, and 894 from *Spanish-American Folk Songs* by Eleanor Hague.

Ascherberg, Hopwood and Crew, Ltd., London: melodies 171, 373, and 387 from *Folk Songs of the North Countrie* by Frank Kidson; melody 341 from *A Garland of English Folk Songs* by Frank Kidson.

Associated Music Publishers, Inc., New York, N.Y.: melody 525 from *Let's Build a Town* by Paul Hindemith, © Copyright 1931, Schott and Co., Ltd. Used by permission of the publisher and Associated Music Publishers, Inc., agents for the United States of America. Melody 1081 from *Das Marienleben* by Paul Hindemith, © Copyright 1923, Schott and Co., Ltd., used by permission of Associated Music Publishers, Inc., agents for the United States of America. Melodies 451, 956, and 966 from *Folk Dance Music of the Slavic Nations,* by H. A. Schimmerling, © Copyright 1951 by Associated Music Publishers, Inc. Melodies 73, 84, 91, 96, 202, 205, 209, 241, 332, 452, 453, and 972 from *Das Lied der Volker* by Heinrich Möller, © Copyright 1929, 1965 by B.Schott's Soehne, Mainz, used by permission of the copyright owner and its agent, Associated Music Publishers, Inc.

C. F. Peters Corporation, New York, N.Y.: melody 811 from *12 Konzert und Opern Arien* by J. C. Bach, copyright C. F. Peters Corporation, 373 Park Avenue South, New York, N.Y., 10016, reprinted with permission of the publishers; melody 606 from *Alte Meister des Bel Canto,* copyright C. F. Peters Corporation, reprinted with permission; melodies 71, 75, 86, 242, 259, 337, 381, 382, and 589 frm *Deutschland im Volkslied* by Gustav Kniep, copyright C. F. Peters Corporation, reprinted with permission.

Columbia University Press, New York, N.Y.: melody 183 from *A Song Catcher in the Southern Mountains* by Dorothy Scarborough.

Elkan-Vogel Co., melody 1060 from *Douze Chants* by Claude Debussy, Durand et Cie of Paris, copyright owners, Elkan-Vogel Company, Philadelphia, sole agents; melody 845 from *Cinq Melodies Popularies Grecques* by Maurice Ravel, Durand et Cie of Paris, copyright owners, Elkan-Vogel Company, Philadelphia, sole agents.

G. Schirmer, Inc., New York, N.Y.: melody 735 from *Anthology of Italian Song* by A Parisotti; mlodies 268, 372, 512, and 566 from *44 French Songs and Variants* by Julien Tiersot; melody 248 from *Reliquary of English Song;* melodies 194, 225, and 1029 from *Songs of Italy* by E. Marzo; melodies 480 and 490 from *Songs of Sweden* by Gustaf Hagg.

Gesellschaft zur Herausgabe von Denkmälern der Tonkunst in Österreich, Vienna: melodies 573 and 1048 from *Denkmäler der Tonkunst in Österreich.*

Harvard University Press, Cambridge, Mass.: melody 778 reprinted by permission of the publishers from *Historical Anthology of Music,* Vol. II, by Willi Apel and Archibald T. Davison, copyright 1950 by the President and Fellows of Harvard College.

Hispanic Institute, New York, N.Y.: melodies 76, 89, 98, 516, 723, 833, 898, 917, 978, and 986 from *Folk Music and Poetry of Spain and Portugal* by Kurt Schindler, courtesy of Hispanic Institute, Columbia University.

H. W. Gray Company, New York, N.Y.; melodies 115, 210, 326, 344, 383, and 536 from *Folk Songs, Chanteys and Singing Games* by Charles Farnsworth and Cecil Sharp, reprinted by permission of Novello & Co., Ltd.

Indiana University Press, Bloomington, Indiana: melody 188 from *Ballads and Songs of Indiana,* edited by Paul G. Brewster.

J. and W. Chester, Ltd., London: melodies 959 and 1082 from *El Retablo de Maese Pedro* by Manuel de Falla, printed by permission of the owners of the copyright, J. and W. Chester, Ltd., London.

Josef Weinberger, Ltd., London: melody 271 from *The Jewels of the Madonna* by Ermano Wolf- Ferrari, copyright Josef Weinberger, Ltd., London; U.S.A. copyright renewed 1961 by Josef Weinberger, Ltd., London.

Librairie Renouard, Paris: melody 316 from *La Musique des Troubadors* by Jean Beck, H. Laurens, éditeur, Paris.

Louisiana State University Press, Baton Rouge: melodies 233, 248, 553, and 784 from *Louisiana-French Folk Songs* by Irene Whitfield.

M. Baron, Company, Oyster Bay, Long Island, N.Y.: melody 801 from *Calypso Songs* by Massie Patterson and Lionel Belasco, copyright 1943 by M. Baron Co.

Novello & Company, Ltd., London: melody 975 from *Caractacus* by Sir Edward Elgar, reproduced by perission of Novello & Co., Ltd., London; melody 844 from *O Lovely Babe* by Alec Rowley, reproduced by permission of Novello & Co., Ltd., London.

Oxford University Press, Inc., London: melody 83 from *Folk Songs from the Southern Appalachians* by Cecil Sharp.

Quintet For Oboe and Strings (measures 55–65) by Merrill Ellis reprinted by permission of Naomi Ellis, copyright owner.

Stainer & Bell, Ltd., Surrey, England: melody 364, "Never Weather-Beaten Sail," by Thomas Campion; melody 964, "Can She Excuse My Wrongs?" by John Dowland; melody 899 from *The Collected Works of William Byrd.*

Theodore Presser Company, Bryn, Mawr, Pa.: melodies 174, 265, 329, and 331 from *Sixty Folk Songs of France* by Julian Tiersot, copyright 1915 by Oliver Ditson, used by permission.

University of Alabama Press, University of Alabama: melodies 342, 475, 484, and 787 from *Folk Songs of Alabama* by Byron Arnold.

University of Arizona Press, Tuscon: melodies 741, 742, and 885 from *Canciones de Mi Padre* (Vol. XVII, No. 1) by Luisa Espinel, by permission of the University of Arizona Press.

University of Utah Press, Salt Lake City: melody 907 from *Ballads and Songs of Utah* by Lester A. Hubbard, University of Utah Press, 1961

Vermont Printing Company, Brattleboro: melodies 228, 734, 812, and 968 from *Concionero Espanol* by Maria Diez de Oñate.

INTRODUCTION

Preparation for Sight Singing

An important attribute of the accomplished musician is the ability to "hear mentally," that is, to know how a given piece of music sounds without recourse to an instrument. Sight singing, together with ear training and other studies in musicianship, helps develop this attribute. The goal of sight singing is the ability to sing *at first sight,* with correct rhythm and pitch, a piece of music previously unknown to the performer. Accomplishing this goal demonstrates that the music symbols on paper were first comprehended mentally before being performed. In contrast, skill in reading music on an instrument often represents an ability to interpret music symbols as fingerings, with no way of demonstrating prior mental comprehension of the score.

Prerequisite to sight singing are some of the simplest aspects of music theory: knowledge of the staff, clef signs, major and minor scales and key signatures, and in rhythm, knowledge of note values and time signatures.

Before reading a given example, make these general preparations (additional instructions for specific problems are included in appropriate chapters):

1. Look at the time signature. Decide what note value receives one beat. How many beats in each measure are there? On what beat of the measure does the example begin?
2. Look at the key signature. What key does it indicate? On what line or space is the tonic of the key ("do" or "1")? Does the melody begin on the tonic

tone or on some other pitch? Play the tonic tone, but no other, immediately before singing.

3. Scan the melody for passages in scale-line movement and then for intervals, particularly those presented in the chapter under study.
4. Observe the phrase marks. The end of a phrase mark usually indicates a cadence, that is, a temporary pause or a final stopping place, much the way commas and periods indicate pauses in language reading. Look ahead to the last note under each phrase mark so that you know where you are heading.
5. The use of the conductor's beat is highly recommended. Use it to help you get all the way through an exercise without stopping. If you make a mistake, don't stop the conductor's beat. The next "one" (the "downbeat") will coincide with the next bar line, where you can pick up your reading and continue. When stopping and repeating, your performance is *not* sight singing! After the first performance, review the exercise and study those places where you made errors.

Practice conductor's beat patterns (shown below) without reading or singing until their use becomes natural enough that you do not have to concentrate on them. Also helpful is the ability to tap with the other hand the division of each beat: in simple time, two taps for each beat, and in compound time, three taps for each beat. For more detailed information, see the author's *Elementary Harmony, Theory and Practice,* third edition, pages 56–61.

The Conductor's Beats: two beats, three beats, and four beats per measure

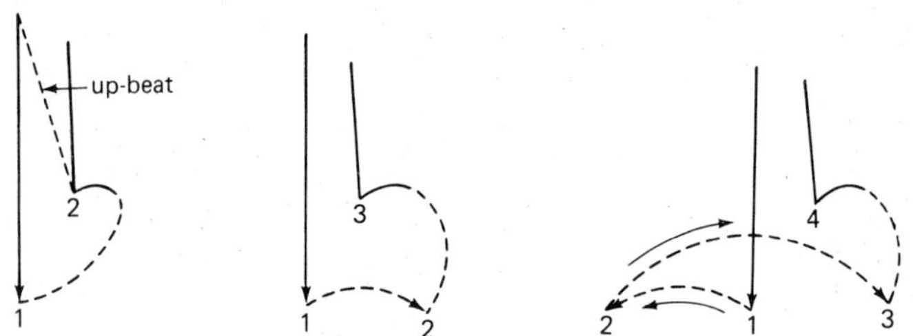

The *downbeat* (one) drops in a straight line and describes a small bounce at the instant the first beat occurs. The first downbeat is preceded by an *upbeat,* beginning at the point of the last beat of the pattern being used. Thereafter, the last beat of each measure is the upbeat for the following measure.

MUSIC
FOR
SIGHT SINGING

CHAPTER 1

MELODY

scale line movement, major keys

RHYTHM

simple time (meter); the beat and its division into two parts

In simple time, the beat is divisible into two equal parts; therefore, any note value so divisible can represent the beat. Most commonly used are the quarter note (♩ = ♫), the eighth note (♪ = ♬), and the half note (𝅗𝅥 = ♩♩), though other values (𝅝, 𝅘𝅥𝅯, 𝅘𝅥𝅰) are sometimes seen. In this chapter, the note value representing the simple division of the beat will be the shortest note value used.

RHYTHMIC READING[1]

Rhythmic reading is best accomplished through the use of rhythmic syllables, as shown in the measures of the example below.

(*a*) Each note value occurring on the beat is read with the number of that beat (measure 1).

(*b*) For a note value longer than one beat, hold the number spoken for the duration of the note value (measures 2, 3).

(*c*) Note values shorter than the beat (appearing other than on the beat) may be read with the syllable "ta" ("tah"), for example, ♫ or as "te" ("tay"), for example, ♫ (measure 3).
one te

[1]An extensive discussion of meter, rhythm, and time signatures, including directions for use of the conductor's beat and hand tapping in rhythmic reading and sight singing, can be found in Chapter 3 of the author's *Elementary Harmony, Theory and Practice,* third edition (Englewood Cliffs, N. J.: Prentice-Hall, Inc., 1983).

(*d*) A rest indicates *silence.* Make no sound (measure 4).

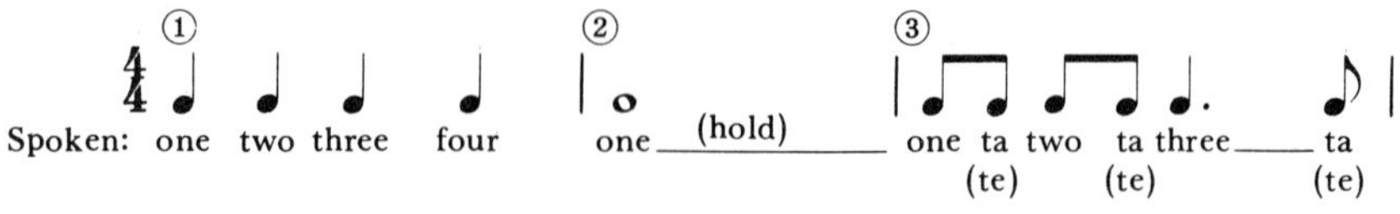

Section 1. The quarter note as the beat unit; undotted note values.

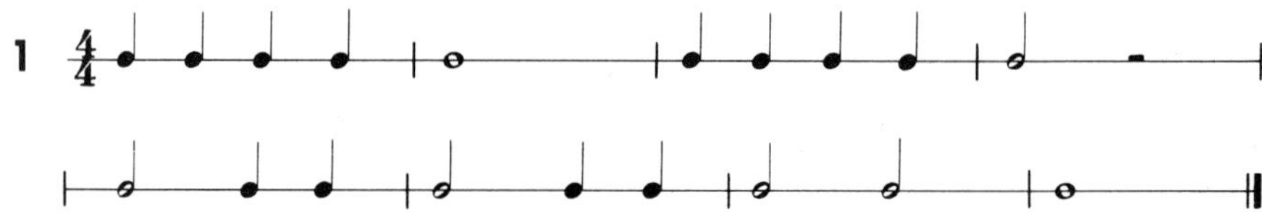

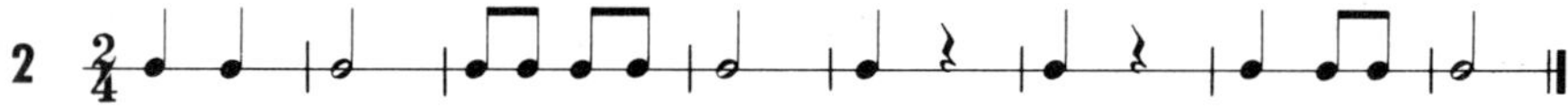

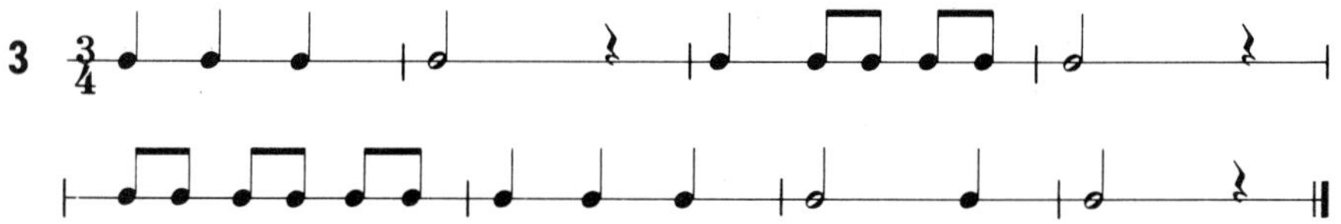

5

6

Section 2. Dotted note values; tied notes.

Section 3. The half note and the eighth note as beat units.

In number 13, examples (*a*), (*b*), and (*c*) sound the same when the duration of each of the beat notes, ♩, 𝅗𝅥, and ♪, is the same.

13

♩ = 1 beat

(A) 4/4

𝅗𝅥 = 1 beat

(B) 4/2

♪ = 1 beat

(C) 4/8

14 4/2

15 3/2

16 2/2

17 ¢

18 4/2

19 4/8

20 4/8

21 3/8

22

23

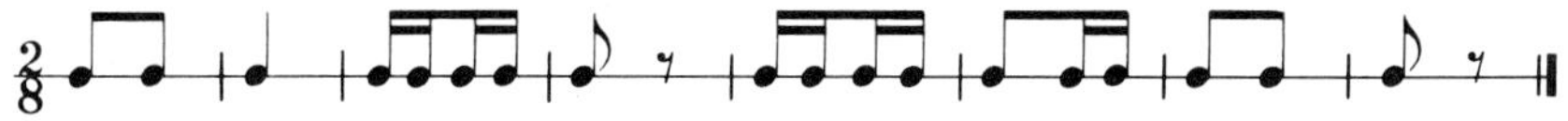

24

Section 4. Two-part drills.

Suggested methods of performance:

1. Two persons: each reads a line.
2. One person: tap both lines, using both hands.
3. One person: recite one line while tapping the other.

25

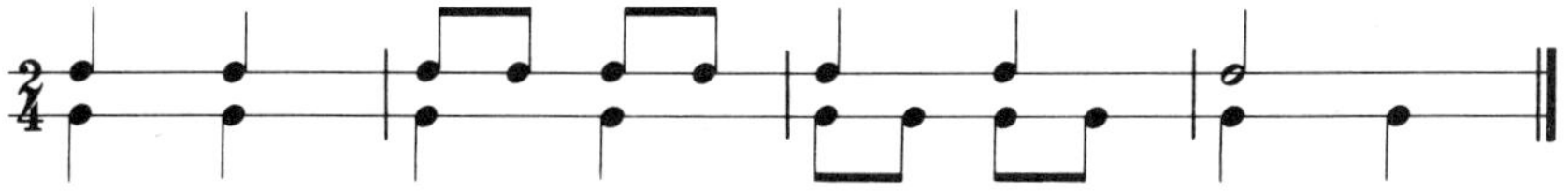

26

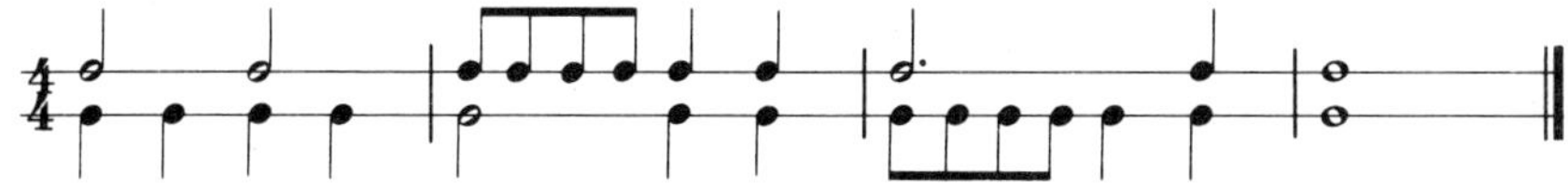

27

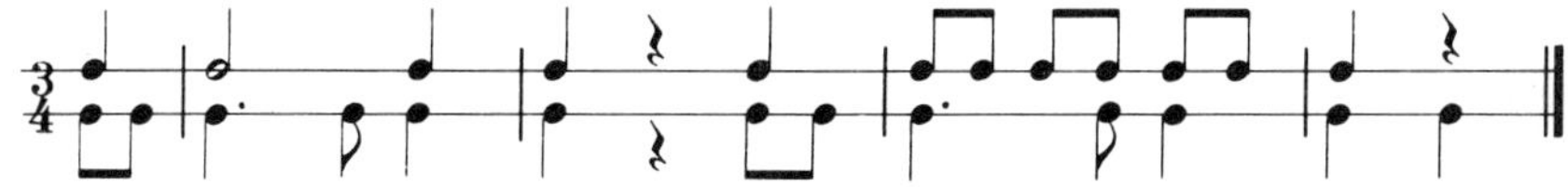

28

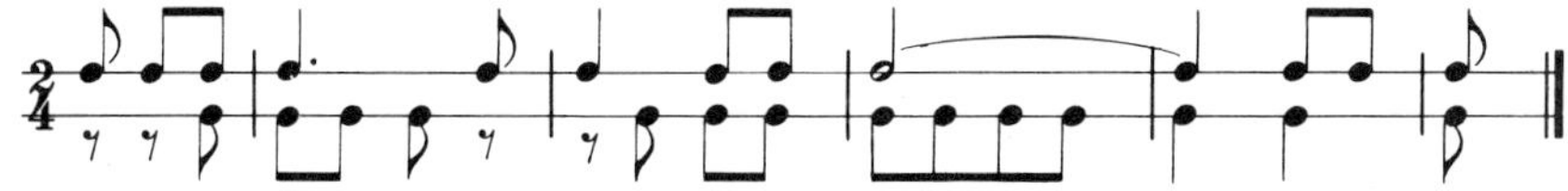

29

30

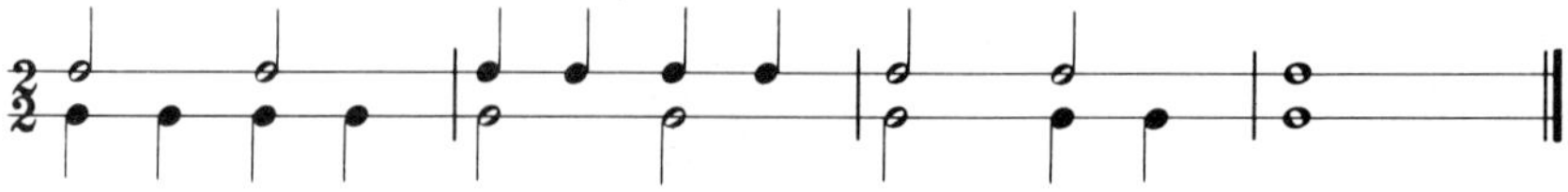

31

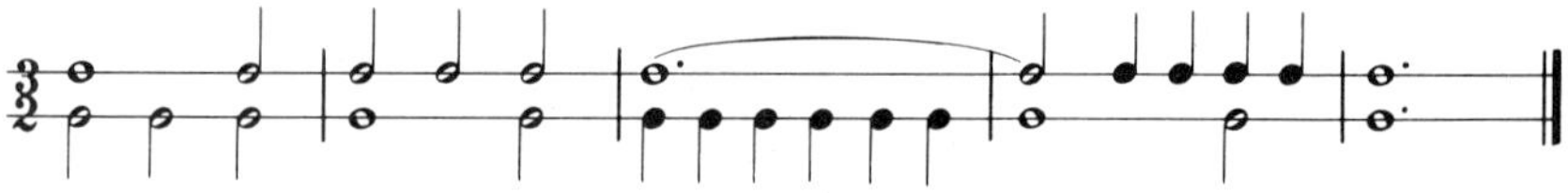

32

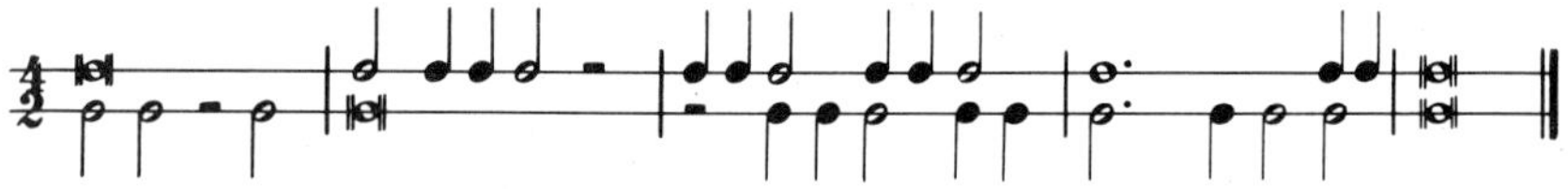

33

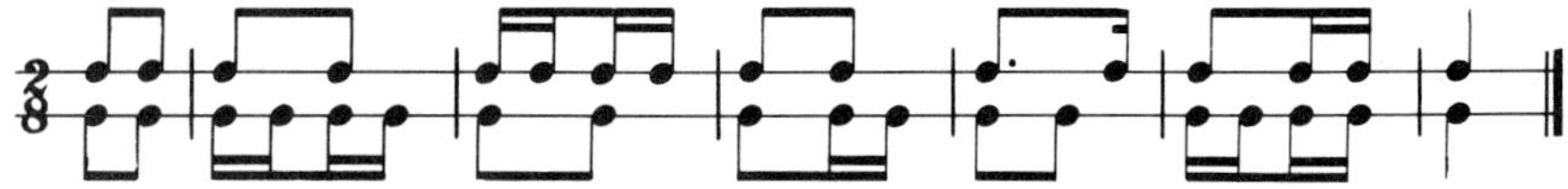

34

35

36

For further practice, read only the rhythm from melodies on the staff, for example:

Melodies from chapters 1 and 2 may be used at this time.

SIGHT SINGING[2]

Several ways to accomplish sight singing are available.

(a) Syllables. In major keys the tonic note is "do," followed by other syllables for each scale step.[3]

(b) Numbers. The tonic note of the key is "1," followed by successive numbers.

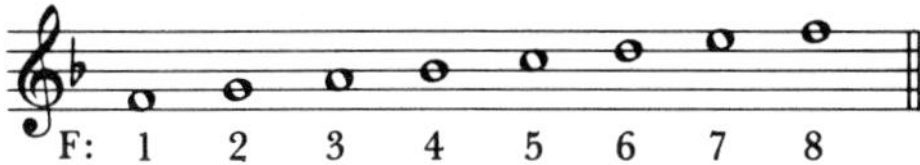

(c) Letter names. Sing each pitch using its staff letter name. When reading both pitch and rhythm, do not add the words "sharp" or "flat," as this changes the rhythm. Saying, for example, "F sharp" on a quarter note produces two eighth notes.

(d) Singing on "la". In this chapter, all melodies will follow a scale line. If you can sing the scale, the use of only "la" should suffice.

Suggested procedure for sight singing.

- (*a*) Read the rhythm as in previous examples.
- (*b*) Locate on the staff the tonic note(s) of the key. In several of following examples, tonic is located by the symbol ⊗.
- (*c*) Sing the scale, ascending and descending, using syllables, numbers, letter names, or "la" as chosen, or as directed by the instructor.
- (*d*) Sing the melody.

[2]Melodies in this chapter were written by the author of the text. The remainder of the text includes only melodies from music literature, but examples from this source occur too infrequently for purposes of Chapter 1.

[3]Known as the *tonic sol-fa* system. In the French *solfège* system, C is always *do,* regardless of the key.

Section 5. Major keys; treble clef; the quarter note as the beat unit.

43

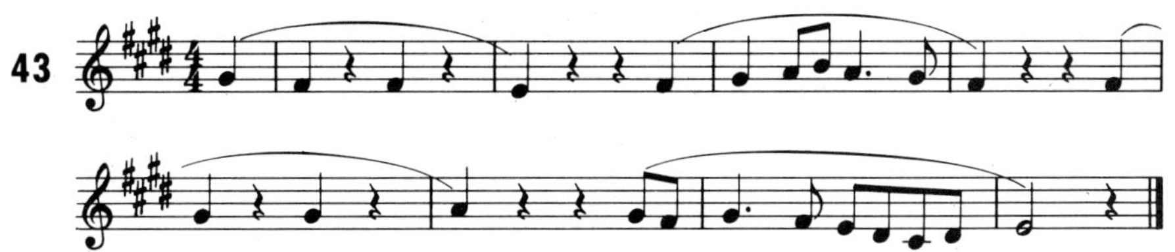

44

Section 6. Bass clef.

45

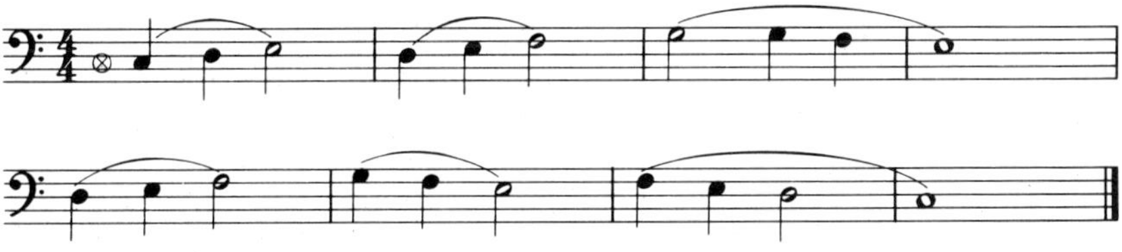

46

47

Section 7. Other time signatures.

54
55
56
57
58
59
60

61

62

Section 8. Duets.

63

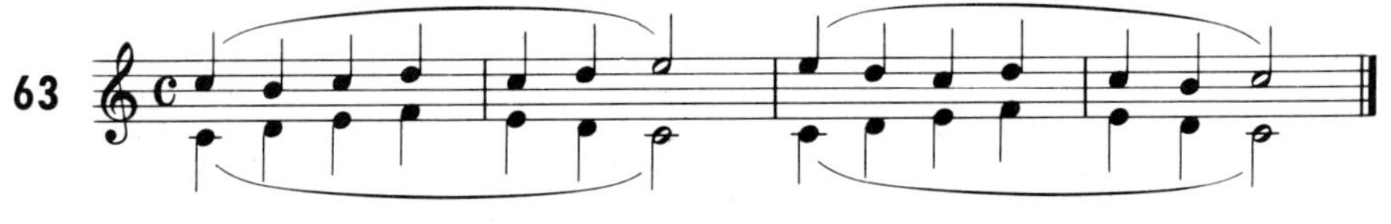

64

65

66

67

68

CHAPTER 2

MELODY

intervals from the tonic triad, major keys

RHYTHM

simple time

The melodies of this chapter contain a wide variety of intervals. The problem of singing these intervals is made easy because they are all readily recognizable parts of the tonic triad. In E♭ major, for example, these intervals are:

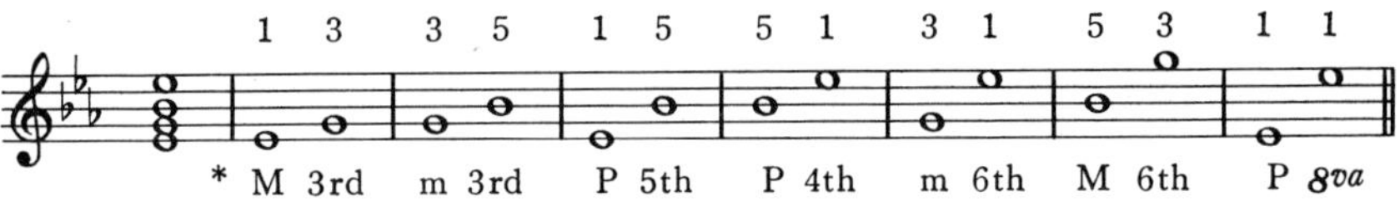

* M=major, m=minor, P=perfect.

Before singing, the following plan of preparation is recommended:

1. Determine the key.
2. Spell the tonic triad.
3. Locate the tonic triad on the staff.
4. Scan the melody for examples of intervals in the tonic triad.
5. Sing the tonic triad.

Try this procedure on the following melody:

Note that:

1. The key is E♭ major.
2. The tonic triad is spelled E♭ G B♭.
3. The tonic triad is located on the first, second, and third lines. Also locate higher and lower tones of the triad on the staff.

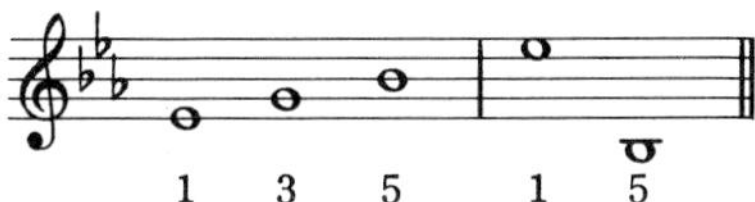

4. Find intervals that are members of this triad. Sing these intervals.

Section 1. Major keys, treble clef, intervals of the third, fourth, fifth and octave from the tonic triad. The quarter note as the beat unit; undotted notes.

70
Moderato
Germany
p
p
71
Allegro
Bavaria
mf
f
dim.
72
Allegro
Spain
mf
73
Allegretto
Poland
74
Allegro
Poland
f
75
Moderato
Silesia
mp

mf
p
rit.
pp
76
Maestoso
Spain
mf
mp
77
Canon for 4 voices
Germany
1
2
3
4
78
Canon for 4 voices
England
1
2
3
4
79
Canon for 3 voices
P. Hayes (18th century)
1
2
3
80
Canon for 3 voices
Caldara (1670–1736)
1
2
3

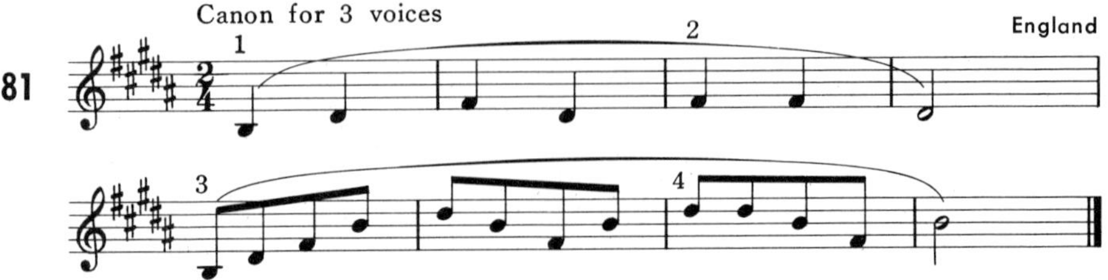

Section 2. Dotted notes.

[1]This melody is from a collection in which Brahms has set folk songs as vocal solos with piano accompaniment. Others will be found on later pages of this text.

Section 3. Bass clef.

Fr. Silcher (1842), Alle Jahre wieder
Allegro
95
mf
f
Allegretto
Spain
96
mf
p
mf
f
Allegro
Händel, Judas Maccabaeus
97
mf
Moderato
Spain
98
f
p
p
Lively
Spain
99
f

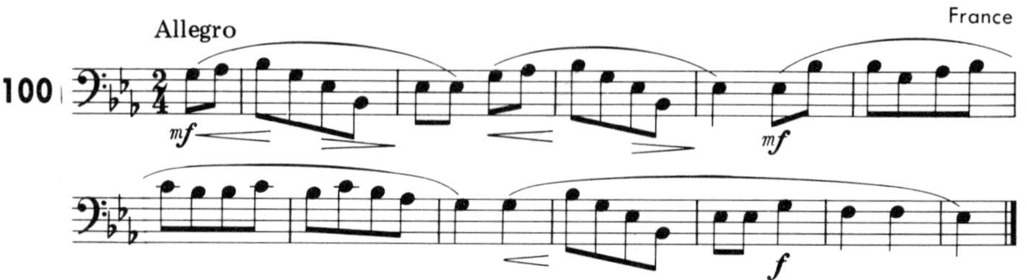

Section 4. Interval of the sixth.

[2]This melody is from a body of folk songs collected by Bartók. Others will be found in later pages of this text.

sp

Allegro
Mexico
104
mp

Allegro moderato
Smetana, The Bartered Bride
105
mf

Moderato
Ohio
106
mf

Canon for 2 voices
Germany
107
1
2

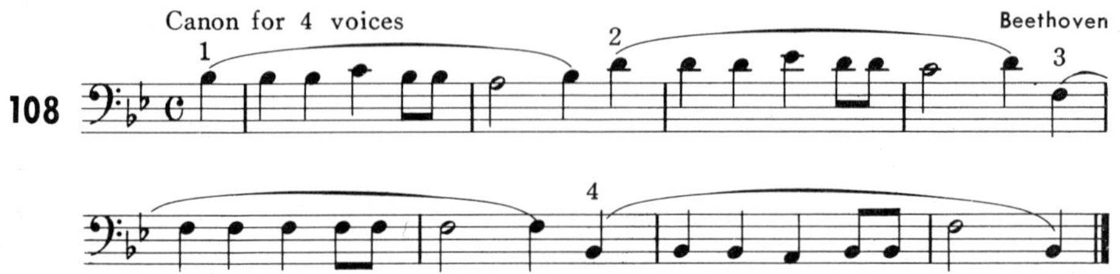

Section 5. The half note and the eighth note as beat units.

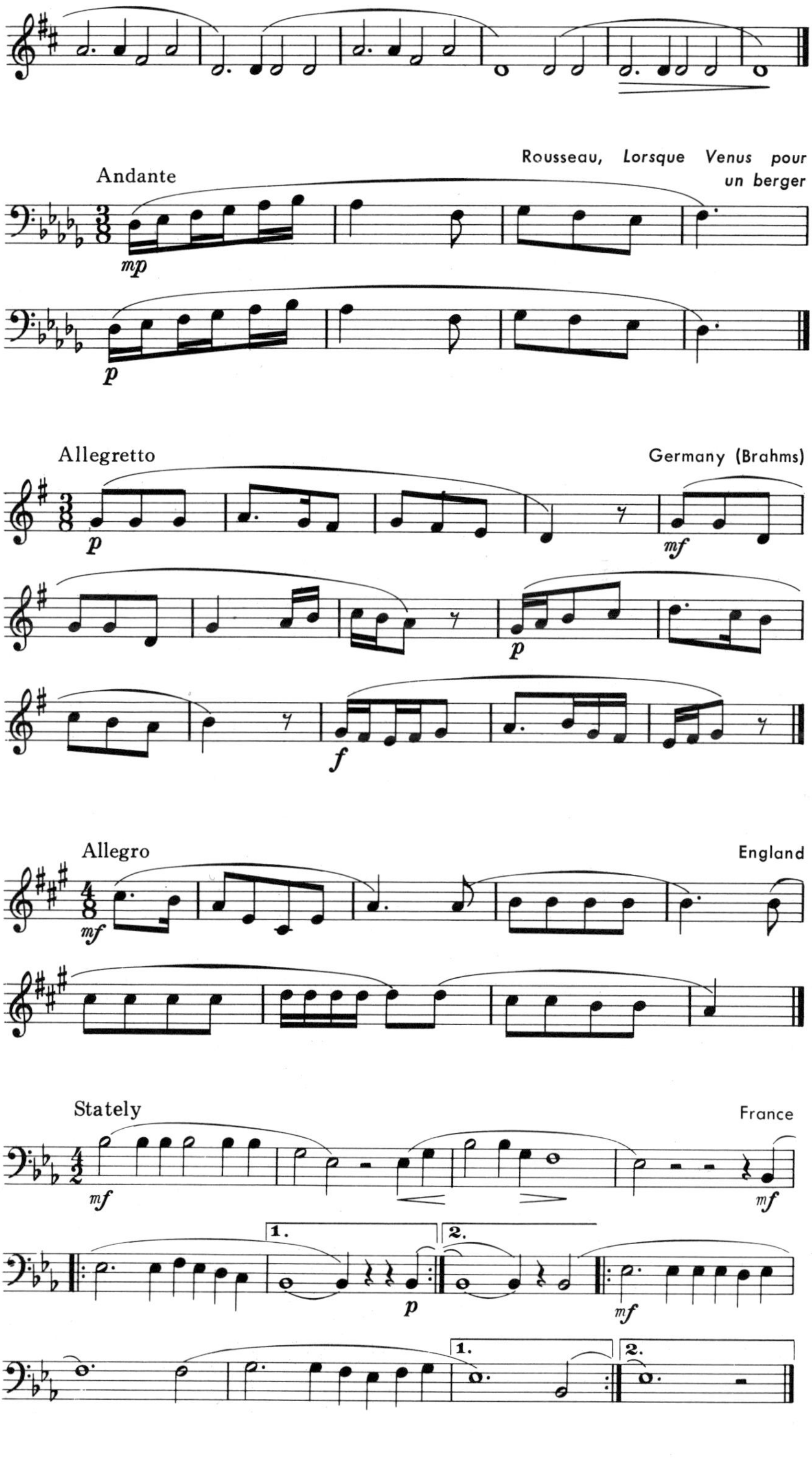

Andante

Rousseau, *Lorsque Venus pour un berger*

113

mp

p

117
Allegretto
Spain
f

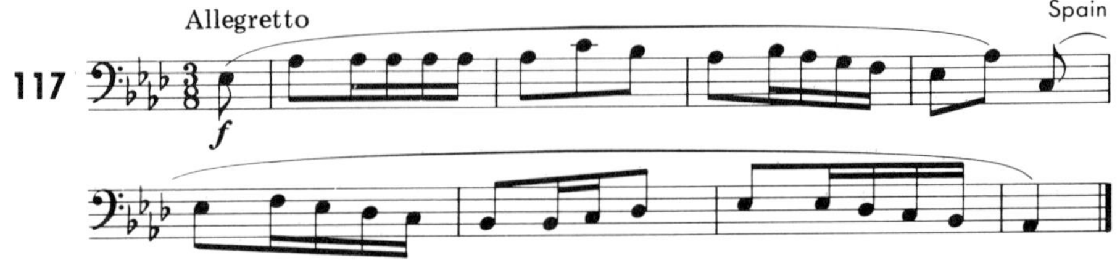

Section 6. Duets.

The asterisk(*) indicates the original folk song, to which a second line has been added.

118
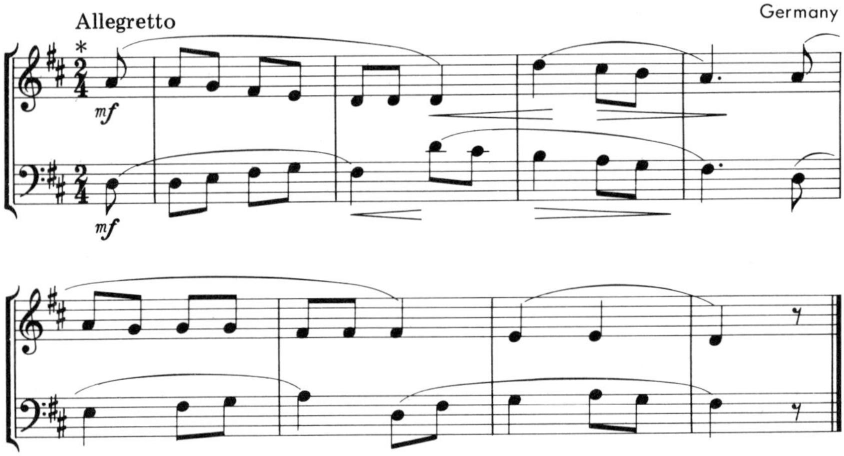
Allegretto
Germany
*
mf
mf

119
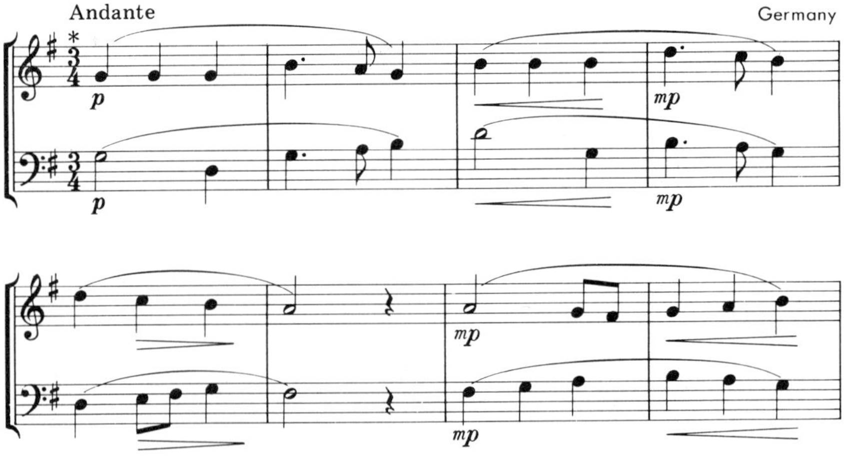
Andante
Germany
*
p
p
mp
mp
mp
mp

mp
mp
mf
mf
Andante
Germany
120
mf
*
mf
mp
mp
Andante con moto
Germany
121
*
mf
mf
Allegro
Germany
122
*
f
f

123 France

124 Largo non troppo Germany

Lively
Germany
125
mf
mp
mp
mf
mp
mf

CHAPTER 3

MELODY

intervals from the tonic triad, major keys

RHYTHM

compound time (meter); the beat and its division into three parts

In compound time, the beat is divisible into three equal parts and therefore is represented by a dotted note value. In $\frac{6}{8}$, for example, the dotted quarter note representing the beat is divisible into three eighth notes (♩. = ♪♪♪). In this chapter, the note value representing the compound division of the beat will be the shortest note value used.

RHYTHMIC READING

Procedures for rhythmic reading in compound time are similar to those in simple time (review page 1). The triple division of the beat may be read with the syllable *ta* ♪♪♪ (one ta ta) or with *la lee* ♪♪♪ (one la lee). The latter is useful when it is desired that the rhythmic syllables differentiate simple and compound time.

Section 1. The dotted quarter note as the beat unit.

126
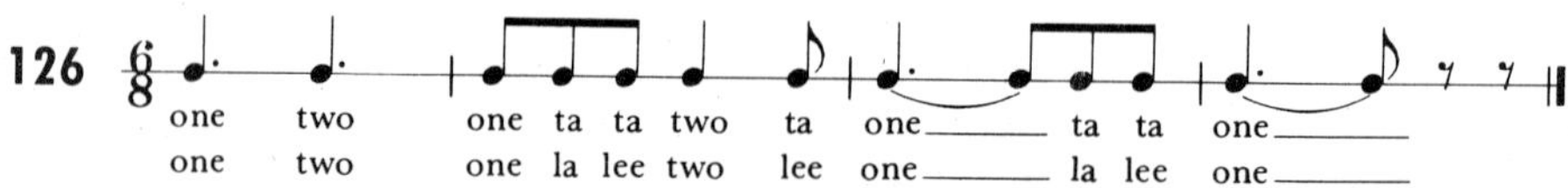

127 6/8

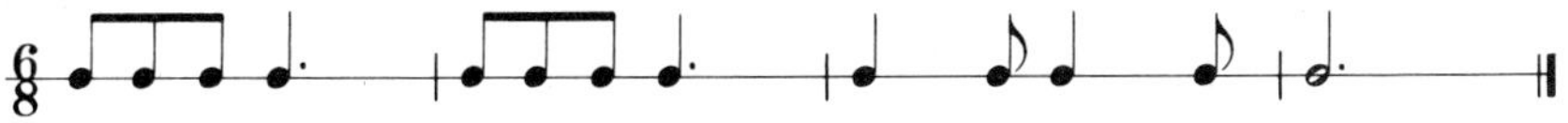

128 6/8

129 6/8

130 6/8

131 6/8

132 9/8

133 9/8

134 9/8

135 12/8

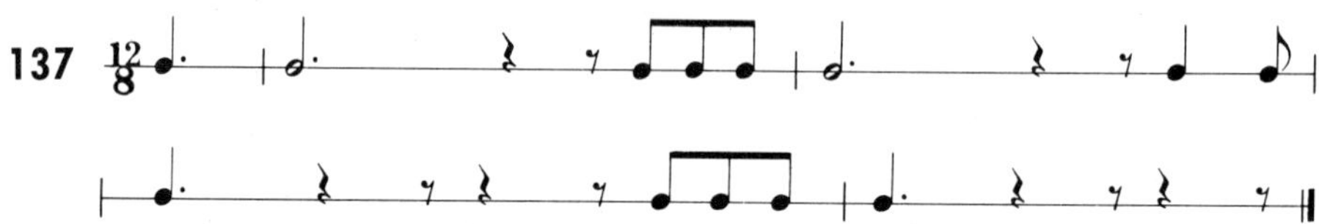

Section 2. The dotted half note and the dotted eighth note as beat units.

In number 138, examples (a), (b), and (c) sound the same when the duration of each of the beat notes, ♩., 𝅗𝅥., ♪., is the same.

138

♩. = 1 beat

(A) 9/8

𝅗𝅥. = 1 beat

(B) 9/4

♪. = 1 beat

(C) 9/16

139 6/4

140 6/4

141 6/4

142 9/4

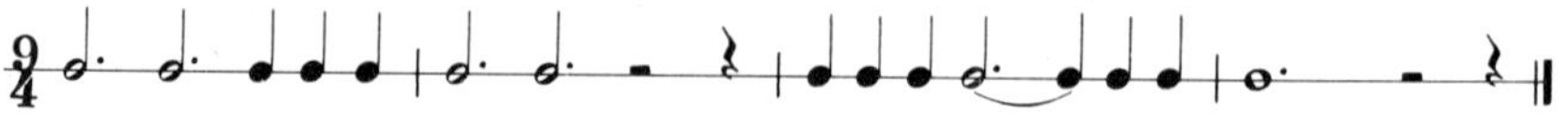

143 9/4

144 9/4

145 12/4

146 12/4

147 12/4

148 6/16

149 6/16

150 6/16

151 9/16

152 9/16

153 9/16

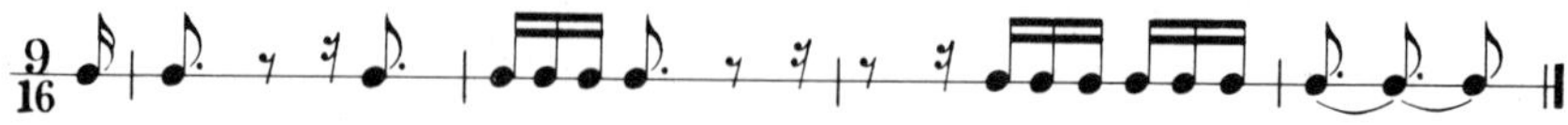

154 12/16

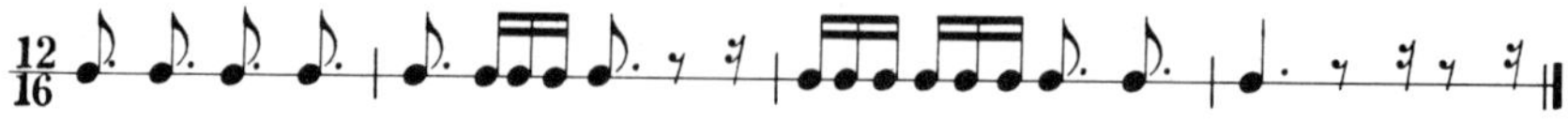

155 12/16

Section 3. Two-part drills.

156 6/8

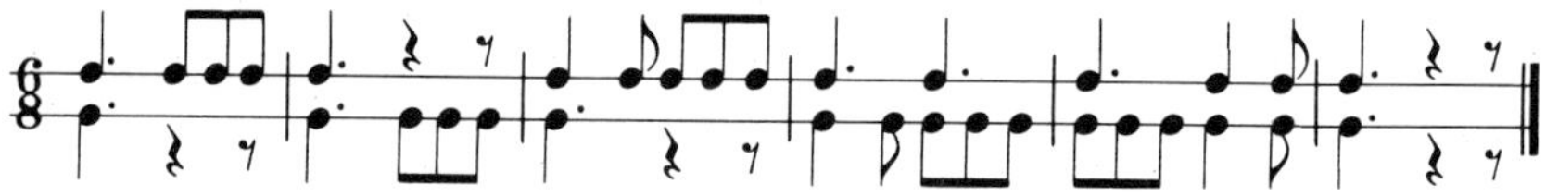

157 6/8

158 9/8

159 9/8

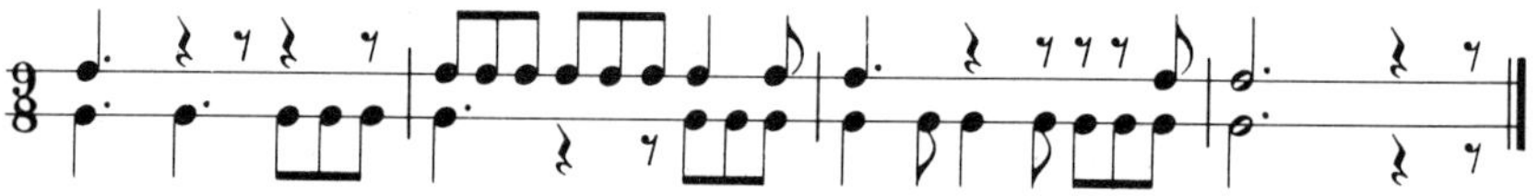

160 12/8

161 6/4

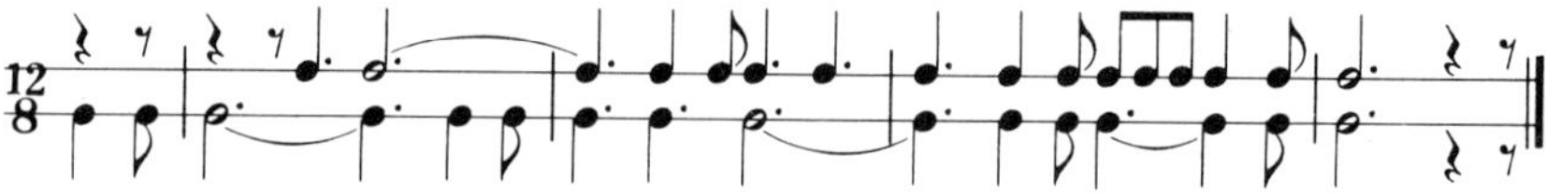

162 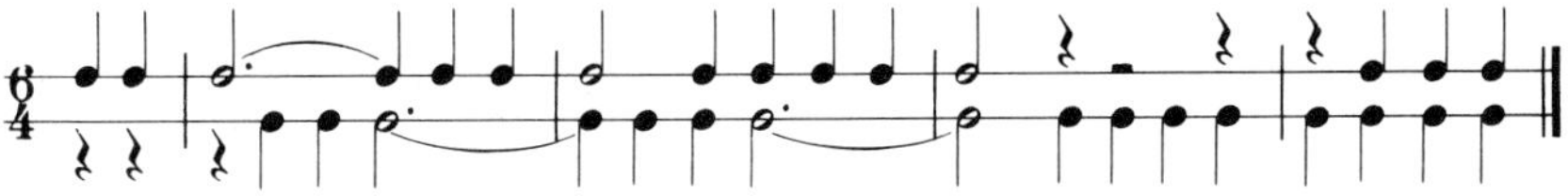

163 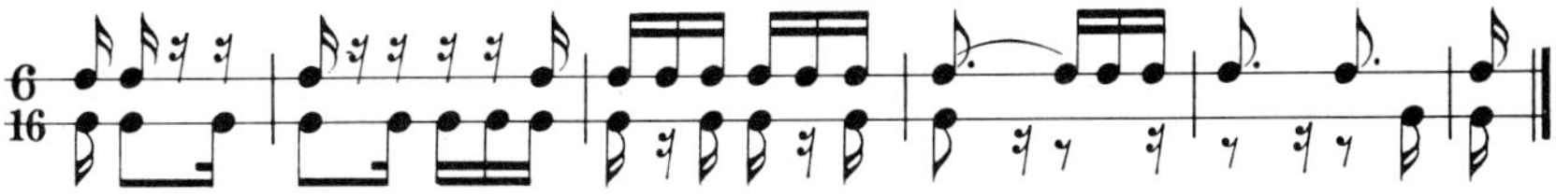

164 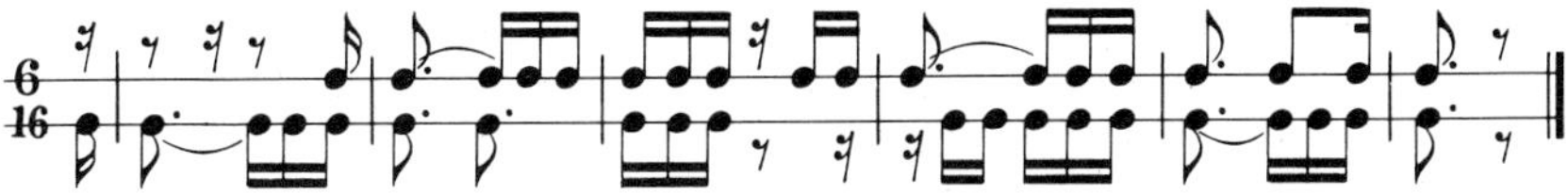

165 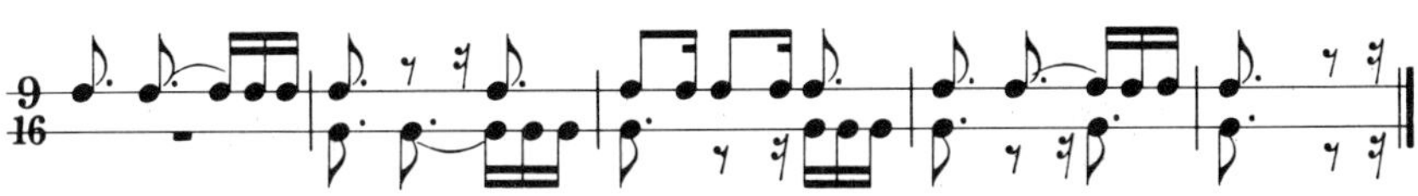

166 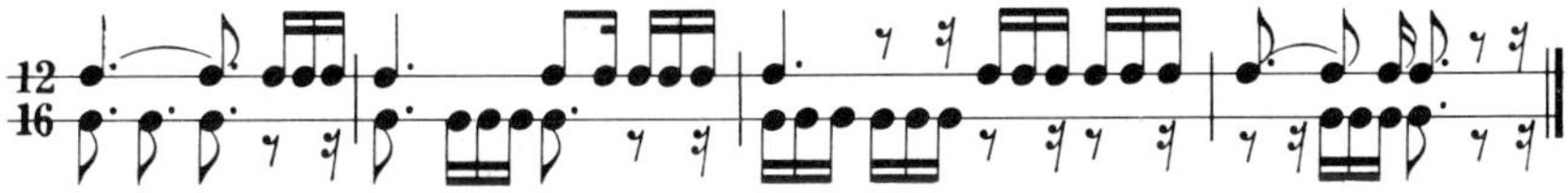

For further practice, read only the rhythm from sight singing melodies in the remainder of this chapter and from the melodies in compound time in Chapter 4.

SIGHT SINGING

Section 4. Major keys; treble clef; the dotted quarter note as the beat unit.

167

168

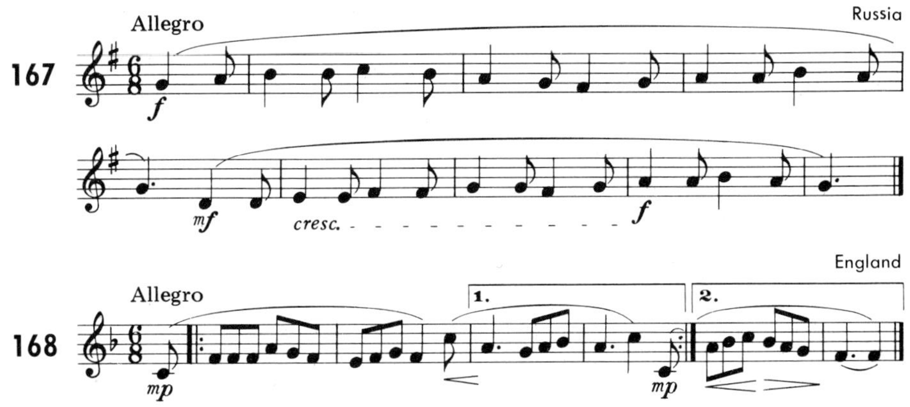

Vif
France
169
mf
f
mf
Moderato
England
170
p
p
Allegro moderato
England
171
mf
mf
Animé
France
172
f

173
Con moto
England
mf

Tchaikovsky, *The Queen of Spades,* Op. 68
174
Allegro vivo
f

175
Con Spirito
England
f
ff

176
Con moto
United States
mf
f
f
mf

Section 5. Bass clef.

Section 6. Other time signatures.

Lively
England
185
f

Moderato
England
186
mf
f
p

Allegretto
France
187
p

Allegretto
Indiana
188
p

Allegro
Germany
189
mp
mp
f
f
Andante
Spain
190
mf
mf

191
Con moto
Germany
f
*
f
mf
cresc.
f
England
192
Moderato comodo
*
1.
2.
mf
mf
193
Allegro
Germany
p
*
p
mf
mf

Allegro moderato
Italy
194
*
6
16
mf
6
16
mf

CHAPTER 4

MELODY

minor keys; intervals from the tonic triad

RHYTHM

simple and compound time

In minor keys, most melodic lines conform to the melodic form of the scale, with scale steps 6 and 7 raised when ascending and lowered (reverting to natural form) when descending.[1]

Before singing, look for the sixth and seventh scale steps of the key and determine whether they are raised or lowered. Example:

Also, watch for these exceptions:

1. A succession of three or more tones, each of which is scale step 6 or 7. The direction of the last tone of the group indicates the scale form for all tones of the group. In melody 197, measure 3, the scale steps are 6–7–6. The final 6 descends; therefore all three tones are from the descending form of the scale (see *Elementary Harmony, Theory and Practice*, pp. 125–127, for further discussion and illustration).

[1]When a melodic line contains an ascending natural seventh scale step, or a raised sixth scale step without an accompanying raised seventh scale step, that line is usually based on one of the medieval modes. See Chapter 15.

2. The tones 7–6–5 descending, with accidentals from the ascending form of the scale. Implied is the use of major dominant harmony. In measure 2 of melody 217 in G minor, the descending melodic line, F♯–E♮–D, implies the use of the V triad, D F♯ A. See *Elementary Harmony, Theory and Practice*, p. 127, for further discussion and illustration.

Sight singing may continue with the use of numbers, letter names, "la," or syllables, as previously chosen. There are two ways in which syllables can be used. The first is the traditional method.

1. The tonic note of the minor scale is la.

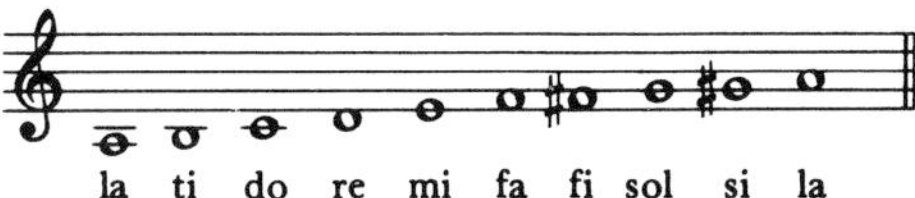

Advantage: The syllables *mi-fa* and *ti-do* locate the half steps both in major scales and in the unaltered steps of minor scales.

Disadvantage: *Do* has already been established as the syllable for the tonic note in major. Using both *do* and *la* for the tonic note can be confusing.

2. The tonic note of the minor scale is do.

Advantage: The tonic of any key, major or minor, is always *do*.

Disadvantage: Syllable names for half steps differ for major and minor scales (major: *mi-fa* and *ti-do;* minor, unaltered scale steps: *re-me* and *sol-le*).

Section 1. Simple time.

Lightly
Germany
196
p

Gracefully and lively
Germany (Brahms)
197
p

Canon for 4 voices
Haydn
198
1
2
3
4

Andante
Germany
199
mp

Allegretto
Germany (Brahms)
200
mp
rit.
p

201
Adagio
England
mp
mf
202
Lento
Finland
mf
mp
mf
pp
203
Canon for 4 voices
England
1
2
3
4
204
Slow
Germany
p
pp
p
mp
pp
205
Moderato
Slovakia
mf
p

206

Allegretto
Slovakia
mp
mf

207

Lento
France
p
pp
p

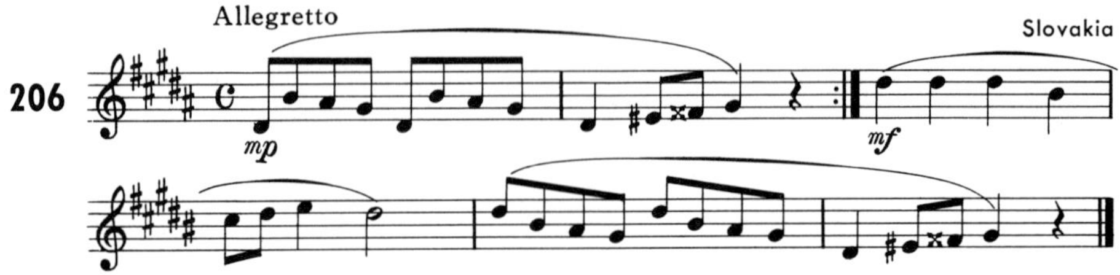

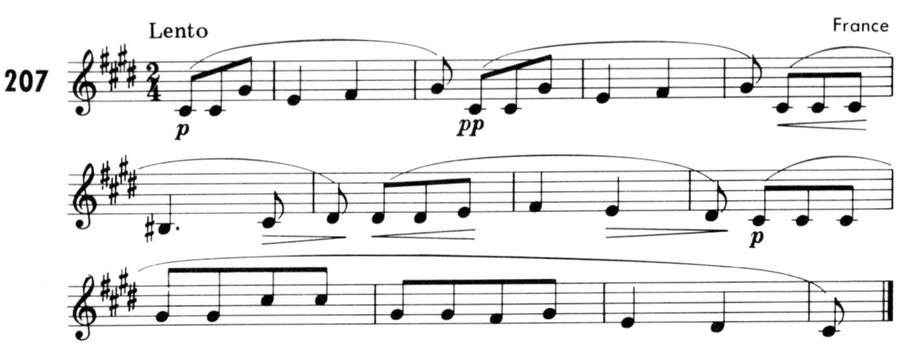

Section 2. Compound time.

208

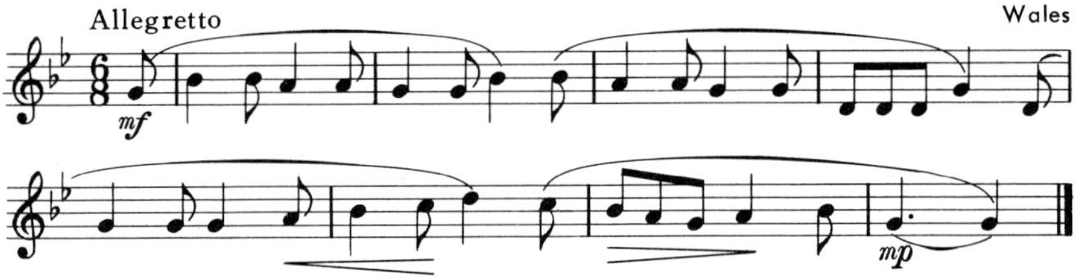
Allegretto
Wales
mf
mp

209

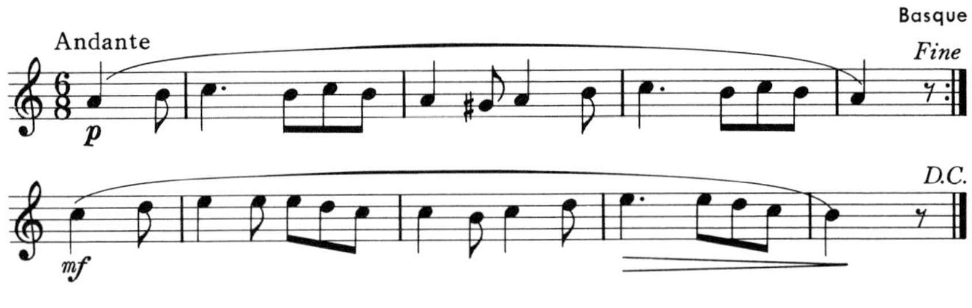
Andante
Basque
Fine
p
D.C.
mf

210

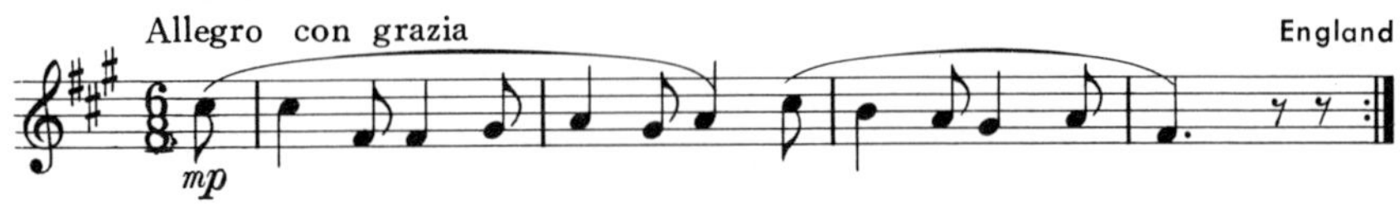
Allegro con grazia
England
mp

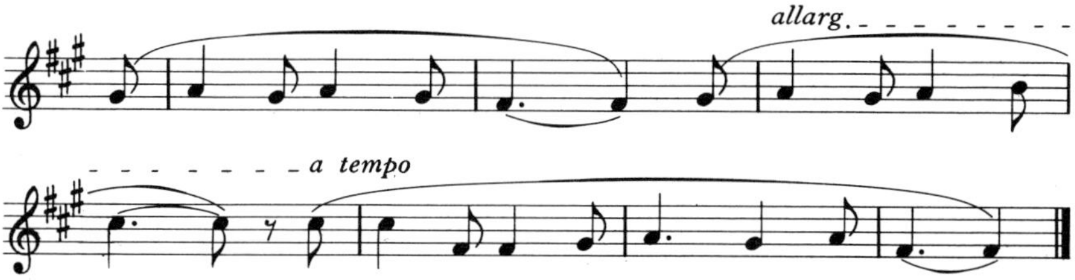
allarg.
a tempo

211 Lento — France

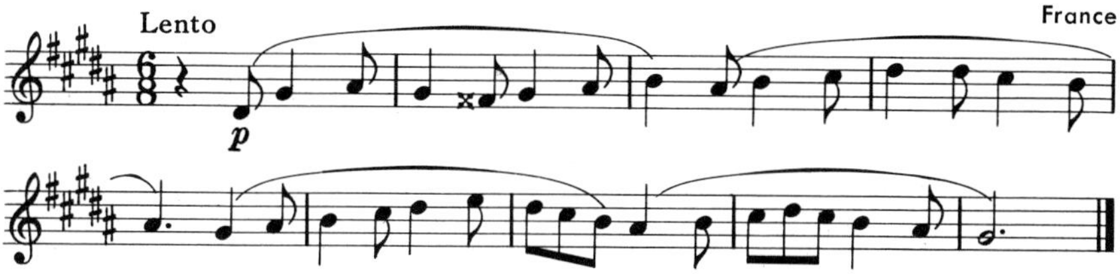
p

212 Allegro — Italy

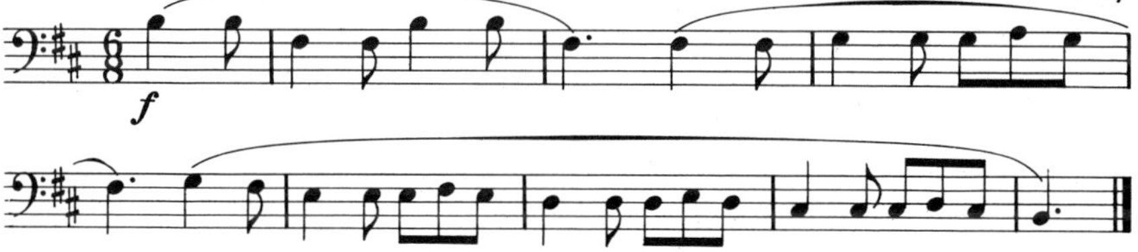
f

213 Larghetto — France

mp
mf
p

214 Allegro — England

mf
f

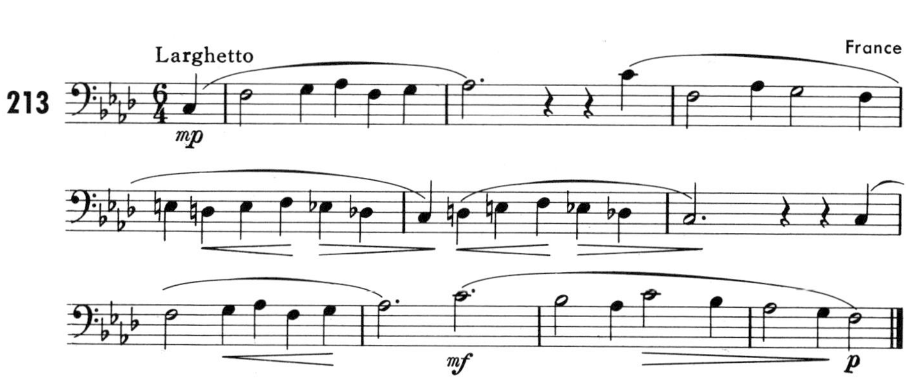

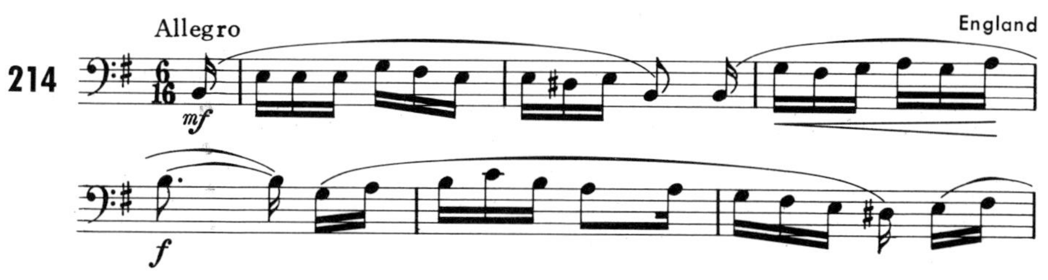

Section 3. Duets.

218
Triste et lent
France
*
pp
pp
mf
mf
pp
pp
219
Adagio
France
*
p
p
220
Moderato
Slovakia
*
mp
mp
cresc.

France
Vif
221
1.
2.
Tristement
France
222

CHAPTER 5

MELODY

intervals from the dominant (V) triad; major and minor keys

RHYTHM

simple and compound time

Intervals from the dominant triad, very common in melodic writing, are the same as those from the tonic triad, but in a different context. Syllable names for members of the V triad are *sol, ti, re* (ascending), and the scale step numbers are 5–7–2, as at (*a*) and (*b*) below. Observe also that its members can be identified as 1–3–5 *of the triad* (*c*).

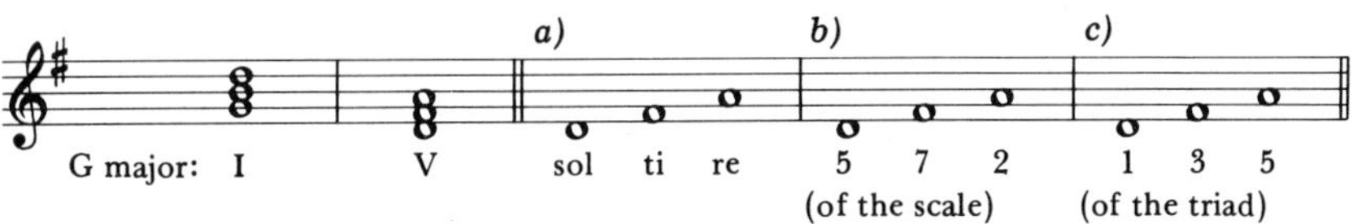

In minor keys, the dominant triad is the same sound as in major keys, since the leading tone is the *raised seventh* scale degree.[1]

[1]Intervallic leaps from the minor dominant triad are uncommon in melodic writing. See *Elementary Harmony*, p. 354, for a discussion of this triad.

Observe these characteristics of the various possible intervals:

1. Skips to the third of the triad (the leading tone) are easy since the second note of the interval, no matter what the size of the interval, is always a half step below the tonic tone.

2. Skips to the root of the triad are easy because this root is the fifth degree (*dominant*) of the scale.

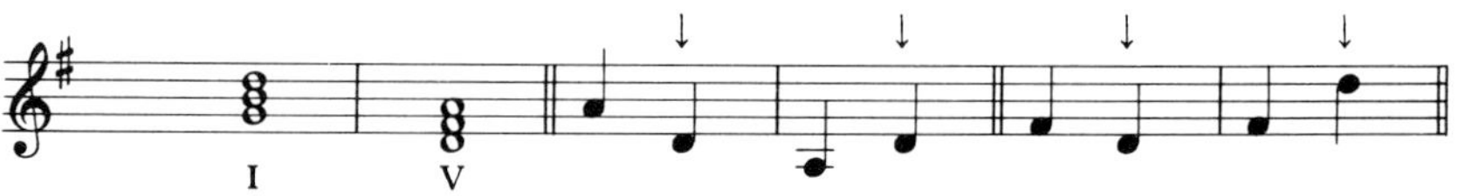

3. Skips to the fifth of the triad are skips to the tone above the tonic (*supertonic*).

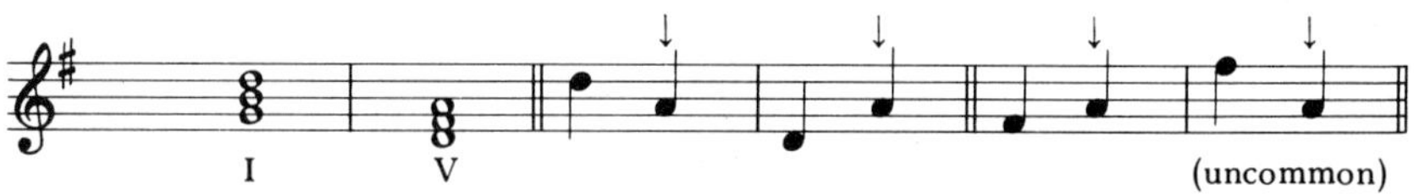

By remembering the sound of the tonic and dominant tones of the key (as learned in Chapters 2–4), any skip in the dominant triad will be either to the dominant tone, or to a scale step above or below the tonic tone.

Before singing, spell the tonic and dominant triads. Then scan the melody for location of intervals from the dominant triad.

Example:

Observe that:

1. The key is G major. I = G B D.
2. The dominant (V) triad is D F♯A.
3. At (*a*) (interval, D down to A), the leap is to the scale step above the tonic tone.
4. At (*b*), the intervals outline the V triad.
5. At (*c*), the interval, though large, is simply a skip to the leading tone, the scale step below the tonic tone.

Section 1. Intervals of the third from the V triad; major keys; simple time.

Allegretto
Lithuania
227
p
mf
(repeat p)
Moderato
England
228
mp
cresc.
p
Allegretto
France
229
mf
p
mf
Con spirito
England
230
Fine
D.C.
Canon for 4 voices
Germany
231
1
2
3
4

Lustily
Germany
232
f
Allegretto
Louisiana
233
mp
Moderato
Germany
234
mf
cresc.
f
Brightly
France
235
f
mp
cresc.
mf
cresc.
f
rit.
a tempo
f

Section 2. Intervals of the third from the V triad; minor keys; simple time.

ff

Mozart, The Abduction from the Seraglio, K. 384
Allegro assai
240
f
pp
cresc.
f

Allegretto
Sweden
241
mp
f
rit.
mp

Andante
Germany
242
mf
p
mf
p

Section 3. Intervals of the fourth and fifth from the V triad; major and minor keys; simple time.

247
Allegro
United States
f
248
Andante
England
1.
2.
p
rit.
a tempo
f
249
Allegro
France
mf
250
Vif
Louisiana
f
rit.
accel. e cresc.

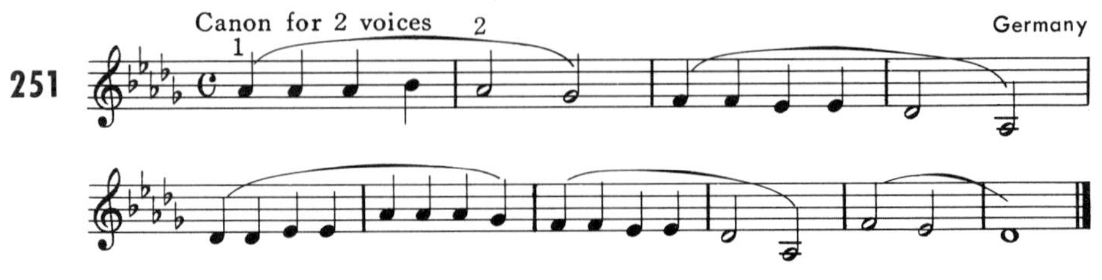
251
Canon for 2 voices
Germany
1
2

252
Canon for 2 voices
Wachsmann (1791–1853)
1
2

253
Ziemlich schnell
Schubert, *Erstarrung*, Op. 89, No. 4
p

254
Andante
Béranger, Ce *jour-là*
p

255
Ruhig
Germany
pp
mp
p
pp

Lebhaft
Germany (Brahms)
256
p

Allegro
Germany (Brahms)
257
p

Lento
Mexico
258
p
1.
2.
mf
p repeat

Andante
Germany
259
mf

Section 4. Interval of the sixth from the V triad; simple time.

Section 5. Various intervals from the V triad; compound time.

269
Andante
Germany (Brahms)
mf
p
mf
p
mf
p

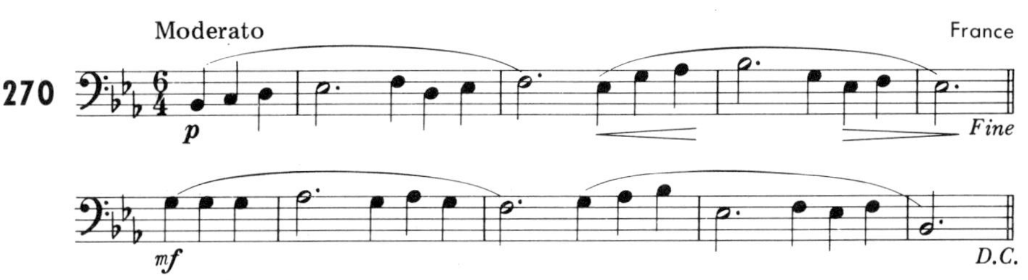
270
Moderato
France
p
Fine
mf
D.C.

271
Presto
Wolf-Ferrari, The Jewels of the Madonna
f

272
Andantino
Massenet, Les Femmes de Magdala
pp très doux

Allegretto

273 Maine

f *p*

Con anima

274 Germany

1. 2. 1. 2.

f

Allegro

275 Germany

Melodies with a numerator of 3 in the time signature, and with fast tempo indications, are very often performed with a single beat per measure. The effect is that of compound time, one beat per measure, as shown in the next four examples.

Fast (𝅗𝅥. = 1 beat)
Germany
276
f
Fine
mf
mf
D.C.
Allegro (♩. = 1 beat)
Germany (Brahms)
277
p
f
rit.
a
tempo
𝅘𝅥𝅮 = 1 beat
Germany
278
mp
1.
2.
Fine
mf
p
D.C.

♩.=1 beat

Canada

279

mf
f
mf
f

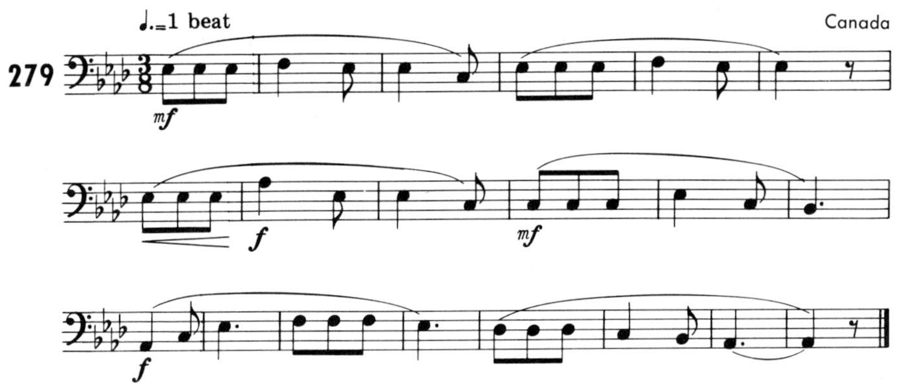

Section 6. Duets.

Lively

Germany

280

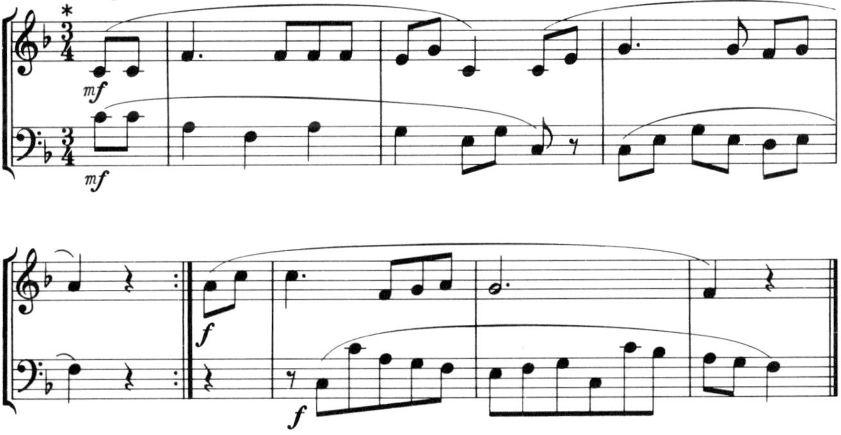

*
mf
mf
f
f

Lebhaft

Austria

281

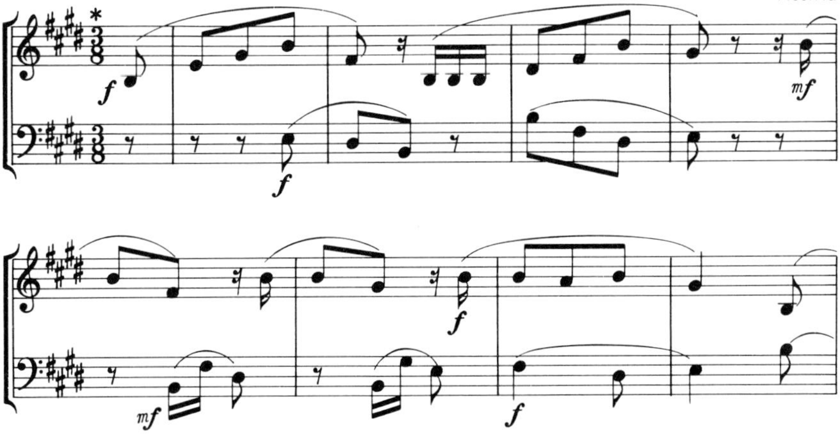

*
f
mf
f
f
mf
f

Allegretto
Canada
282
Lentement
France
283

284
Allegro con brio
Netherlands
mf
*
mf
f
mf
f
mf
285
Largo
Netherlands
mp
*
mp
cresc.
cresc.
mf
mp
mf
p
p
286
Andante
Netherlands
*
mf
mf

f
mf
f
mf
f
f

CHAPTER 6

THE C CLEFS

alto and tenor clefs

The clef sign or, 𝄡 less commonly, 𝄡 indicates the location of *middle C* on the staff. When found on the third line of the staff, the C clef is known as the "alto clef"; when found on the fourth line, it is known as the "tenor clef."

Alto clef

Tenor clef

The alto clef is commonly used by the viola, and the tenor clef is used by the cello, trombone, and bassoon.

The music of this chapter involves a review of the problems of the previous chapters. Each example is in either the alto or tenor clef. Further study in C-clef sight singing can be done by means of clef transposition of any melody in the treble or bass clef. To illustrate, let us take melody 83 from Chapter 2, which begins as follows:

First, observe that the tonic note of the key is on the second line. Next, cover the treble clef sign and the key signature; visualize in its place an alto clef. When using the alto clef, you will find that the second line on the staff is A; therefore, in the alto clef, this melody will be in the key of A major. Then, by visualizing an alto clef and a key signature of three sharps, you can sing the melody in the key of A major (or, with four flats, in the key of A♭ major).

The same procedure can be used for the tenor clef. Because the second line in the tenor clef is F, the melody can be sung in the key of F major (or F♯ major).

When the melody does not start on the tonic, be sure to find the tonic note of the original melody and work from that note when transposing. For example, in melody 72 in Chapter 2:

To facilitate learning the C clefs, these melodies should be read using letter names (but without the words "sharp" or "flat") regardless of the system used in previous chapters.

Two other C clefs and one F clef, which are rarely used in printed music today, can be utilized for transposition. They are:

These three plus the treble, bass, alto, and tenor clefs comprise a group of seven clefs by which any pitch name can be transposed to any other pitch name. Adding appropriate accidentals will give any major or minor key signature.

Section 1. The alto clef.

The pitches of versions (a) and (b) of melody 287 are identical.

287 (a) **Andante** — England

mf

(b) **Andante**

mf

288 Allegretto — England

mf

289 Andante — England

p

290 Canon for 4 voices — Hauptmann (1792–1868)

1 2 3 4

291 Canon for 4 voices — Webbe (c. 1680)

1 2 3 4

Moderato
Germany
292
mf
Lively
Mexico
293
mp
f
Lively
Netherlands
294
f
1.
2.
Allegro
Germany
295
f
mp
mf
f

Andante
Poland
296
f

Andante
Germany (Brahms)
297
p
mf
pp
p

Schubert, Der Musensohn, Op. 92, No. 1
Allegro
298
mf
mp
mf

Allegro
Italy
299
mp

Allegretto
France
300
f
Moderato
Germany
301
p
Andante con moto
Germany
302
mp
mp
mf
mf

303
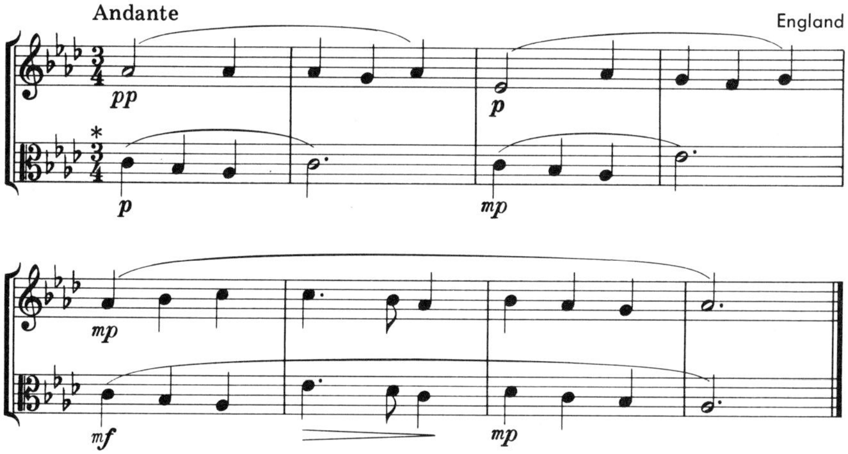
Andante
England
pp
p
p
mp
mp
mf
mp

304
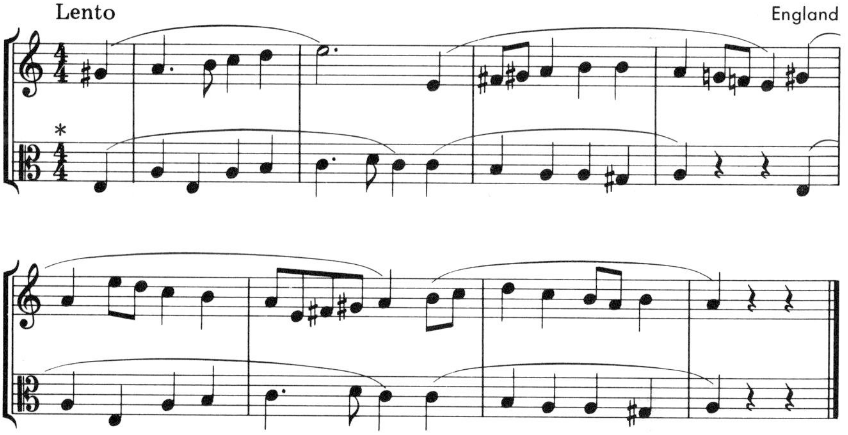
Lento
England

Section 2. The tenor clef.

The pitches of versions (a) and (b) of melody 305 are identical.

305
(a)
Allegretto
England
p

(b)
Allegretto
p

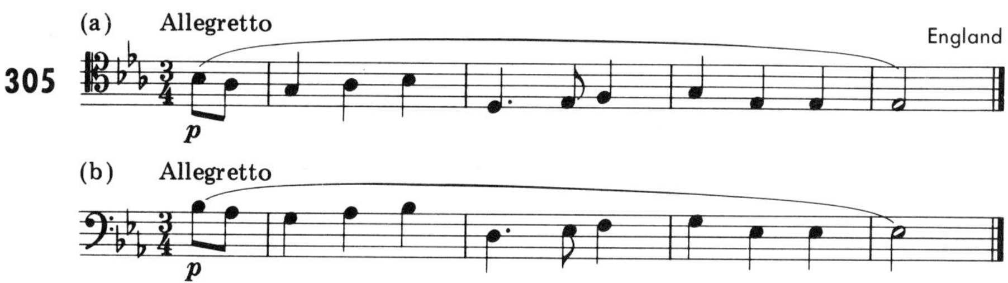

306
Maestoso
Germany
f
307
Allegretto
England
f
mp
rit.
308
Canon for 4 voices
England
1
2
3
4
309
Animé
France
f
p
310
Lively
Germany
f

Canon for 4 voices
England
311
Canon for 4 voices
Brahms
312
Andantino
Germany
313
mp
mf
1.
2.
Canon for 4 voices
Praetorius
314

Allegro

England

317

mf

*

f

sp

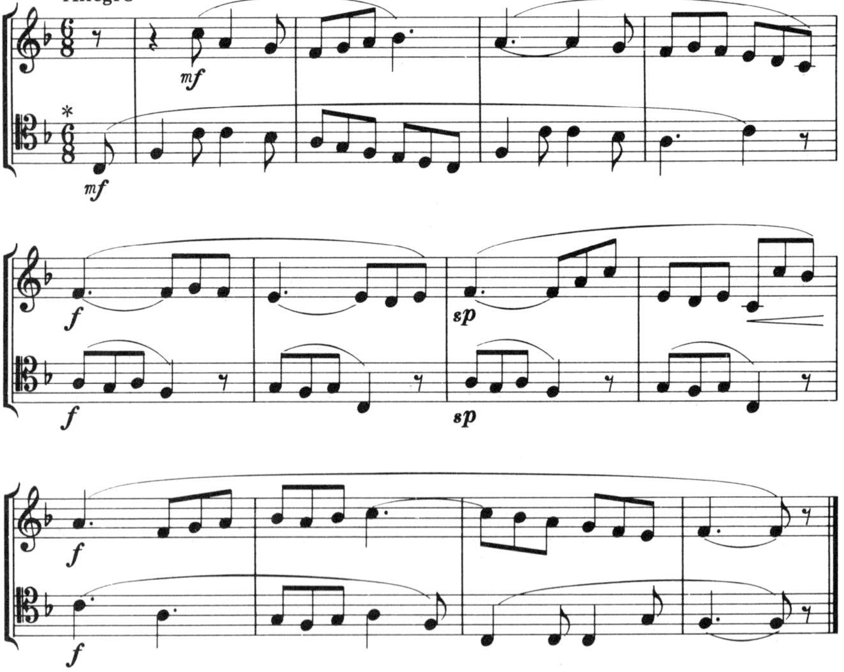

318

CHAPTER 7

MELODY
further use of diatonic intervals

RHYTHM
simple and compound time

Those intervals found as members of the tonic and dominant triads can also be found in several other contexts, several of which are presented in this chapter. Having already learned these intervals from the preceding chapters, they should present little difficulty in their new contexts.

Section 1. The minor third between the second and fourth scale steps, implying the dominant seventh (V^7) chord.

The use of this minor third is very common in melodic writing. It usually implies chord members 5 and 7 (or the reverse) in the dominant seventh (V^7) chord, a chord containing several new intervals and to be presented formally in Chapter 10. Because of the ease in singing this simple interval, it is not necessary to understand its derivation and function at this time.

Rather fast
Kentucky
319
Moderato
Germany
320
Canon for 4 voices
Germany
321
1.
2.
3.
4.
Canon for 4 voices
Hauptmann
322
1
2
3
4
Canon for 3 voices
Caldara
323
1
2
3

324
Canon for 4 voices
Germany
1
2
3
4
325
Allegro
Handel, Judas Maccabaeus
f
ff
mf
cresc.
f
326
Moderato
England
f
327
Allegro
England
f
rit. - - - - - - - - - - - a
tempo

Spain
Allegretto
328
1.
2.
France
Lento
329
Allegro
Massenet, Première Danse
330
Pas trop lent
France
331

Andante
Denmark
332
mf
rit.
Allegro (♩. = 1 beat)
Mozart, Divertimento No. 2, K. 131
333
mf
Canon for 3 voices (♩. = 1 beat)
Anonymous
334
1
2
3

Section 2. Intervals implying the IV and ii triads.

A series of two notes may clearly imply, or a series of three notes clearly outline, either of these triads. Melodies 337–346 demonstrate intervals from the IV triad; melodies 347–353 demonstrate those from the ii triad.[1]

[1]See Section 3 for additional melodies. Many contain intervals which seem to imply IV or ii but which function otherwise, as explained in the introduction to Section 3.

338
Allegro
Germany
f
339
Langsam
Schubert, Morgenlied
pp
340
Canon for 3 voices
England
1
2
3
341
Andante
England
p
cresc.
p
342
Allegretto
Alabama
f

343
Con spirito
Germany
f
344
Allegro moderato
England
mf
345
Gaily
Germany (Brahms)
p
346
Moderato
France
mf
347
Moderato
Germany
1.
2.
p
348
Allegretto
Poland
mf
f
sfz
cresc.

Allegro
Germany
349
mf
Beethoven, Quartet No. 16, Op. 135
Lento
350
p
p
p
p
Haydn, Symphony No. 100
Presto
351
p
Schubert
Canon for 3 voices
1
352
2
3
Mendelssohn, Das Schifflein, Op. 99, No. 4
Andante con moto
353
p

Section 3. Other intervallic implications.

At times, an interval may not suggest a single harmony:

a. Each note of the interval may imply a different harmony; or
b. Either note of the interval (usually the second) may be a nonharmonic tone.

Both of these conditions can be demonstrated in melody 365.

When combining the measures above with measures 9–10, as heard when performing the canon, the harmonic context is complete and these uses of intervals can be seen clearly.

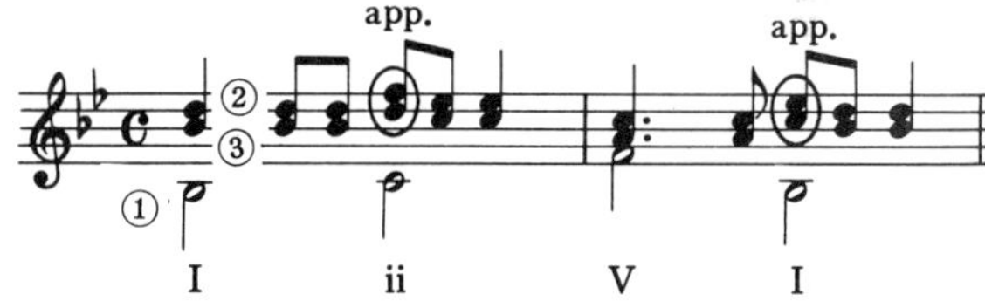

Beethoven, Mit einem gemalten Band, Op. 88
Lightly
355
pp
sempre

Canon for 3 voices
Haydn
356
1
2
3

Canon for 3 voices
England
357
1
2
3

Allegretto
Germany
358
mp

359

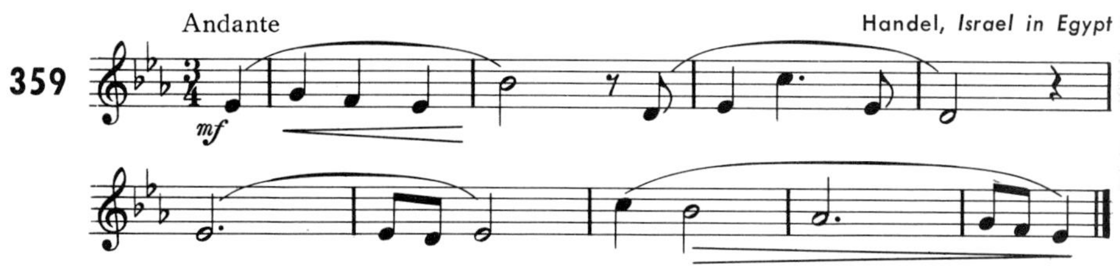

360

361

362

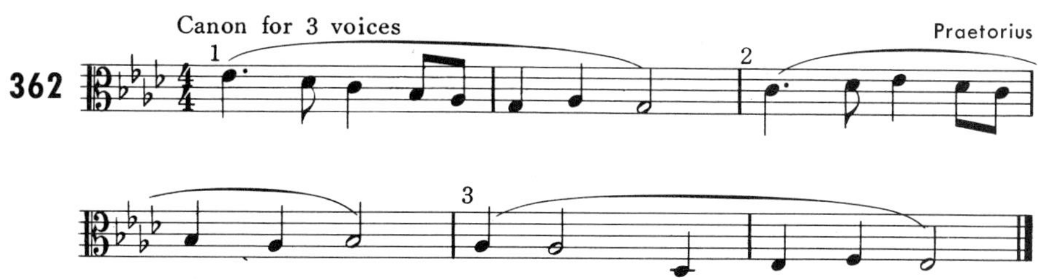

363
Canon for 3 voices
England
1
2
3
364
Andante
Campion (16th century), *Never Weather-Beaten Sail*
p
mf
p
cresc.
mf
365
Canon for 3 voices
Mozart
1
2
3

366
Canon for 4 voices
Germany
1
2
3
4
367
Canon for 3 voices
England
1
2
3
368
Moderato
Germany
f
Fine
mf
f
D.C.

369 

370 

371 

* From *Americans and Their Songs* by Frank Luther, 120 E. 56th Street, New York 22, N.Y.

372 

Moderato
England
373
mf

Canon for 3 voices
Schubert
374
1
2
3

Slowly
Bahamas
375
p
cresc.
mf
p

Andante sostenuto
Massenet, Chant Provencal
376
p
dolce
poco rit.

Andante
Germany
377
mp
Moderato
Schubert, Der Entfernten
378
mf
Bien allant
France
379
mf
Moderato
England
380
mf

Adagio
Westphalia
381
p
p
mp
mf
mf
p
p
Andante
Silesia
382
mf
mf
Con moto
England
383
mf
mf
f
f

mf
mf
Andante con moto
Germany
384
mp
mp
mf
mf
f
f
Adagio
England
385
p
p
mf
mf
p
p

Allegro vivace assai
Mozart, Quartet, K. 458
386
f
f
Allegro
Mozart, The Magic Flute, K. 620
387
p
p
dim.
dim.

CHAPTER 8

RHYTHM

the subdivision of the beat: the simple beat into four parts; the compound beat into six parts

RHYTHMIC READING, SIMPLE TIME

In simple time, the beat may be subdivided into four parts—for example, 2/4 ♩ = ♬♬, 2/2 𝅗𝅥 = ♫♫, 3/8 ♪ = ♬♬, and so forth.

Rhythmic syllables may be used as follows:

(a) All note values shorter than the beat note may be read using the syllable "ta."

(b) When using the syllable "te" for the divided beat, note values shorter than "te" are read using "ta."

Section 1. Preliminary exercises, simple time.

Read each line, repeating without interrupting the tempo, until it is mastered. Continue in a like manner with the following line. When all lines are completed, skip from one line to any other line, as directed or as chosen, without interrupting the tempo.

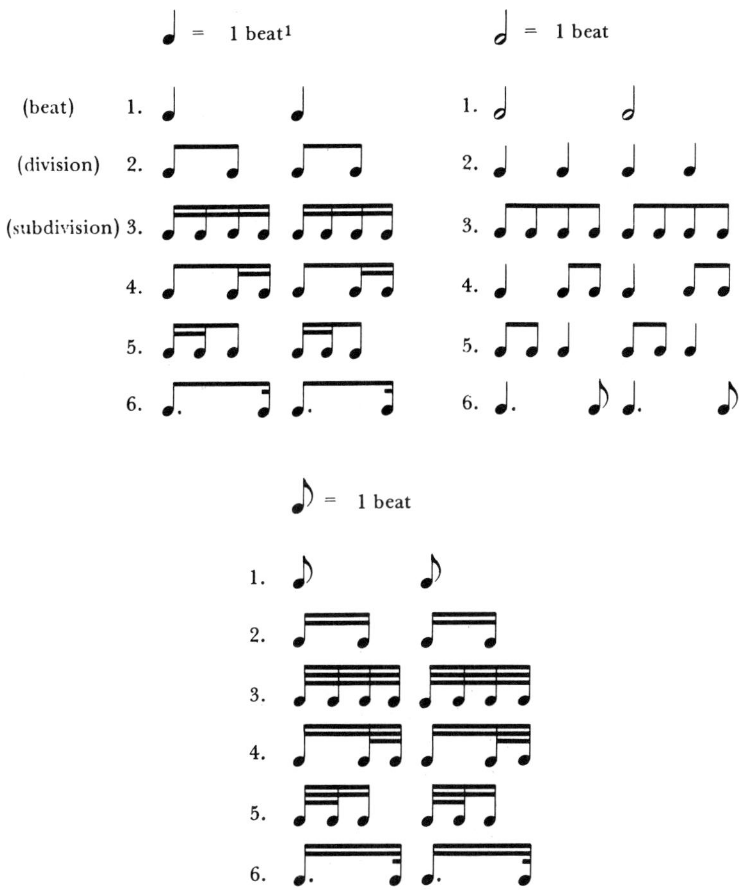

♩ = 1 beat[1]

(beat) 1.

(division) 2.

(subdivision) 3.

4.

5.

6.

𝅗𝅥 = 1 beat

1.

2.

3.

4.

5.

6.

♪ = 1 beat

1.

2.

3.

4.

5.

6.

Section 2. Rhythmic reading exercises in simple time.

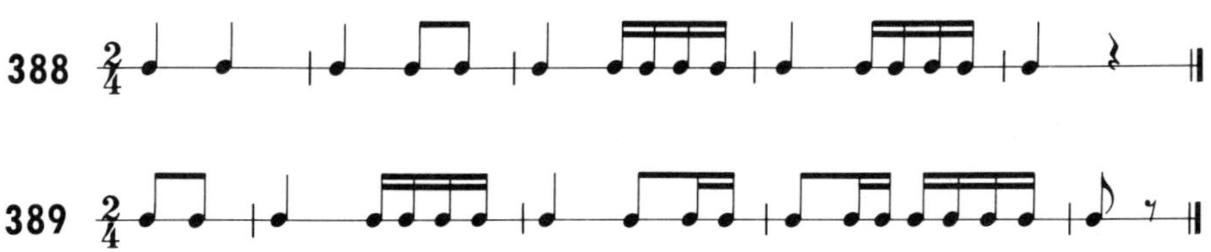

[1]See Chapter 14 for the rhythmic figures ♪♩. and ♪♩♪ (when ♩ = one beat) and comparable figures (for other beat-note values).

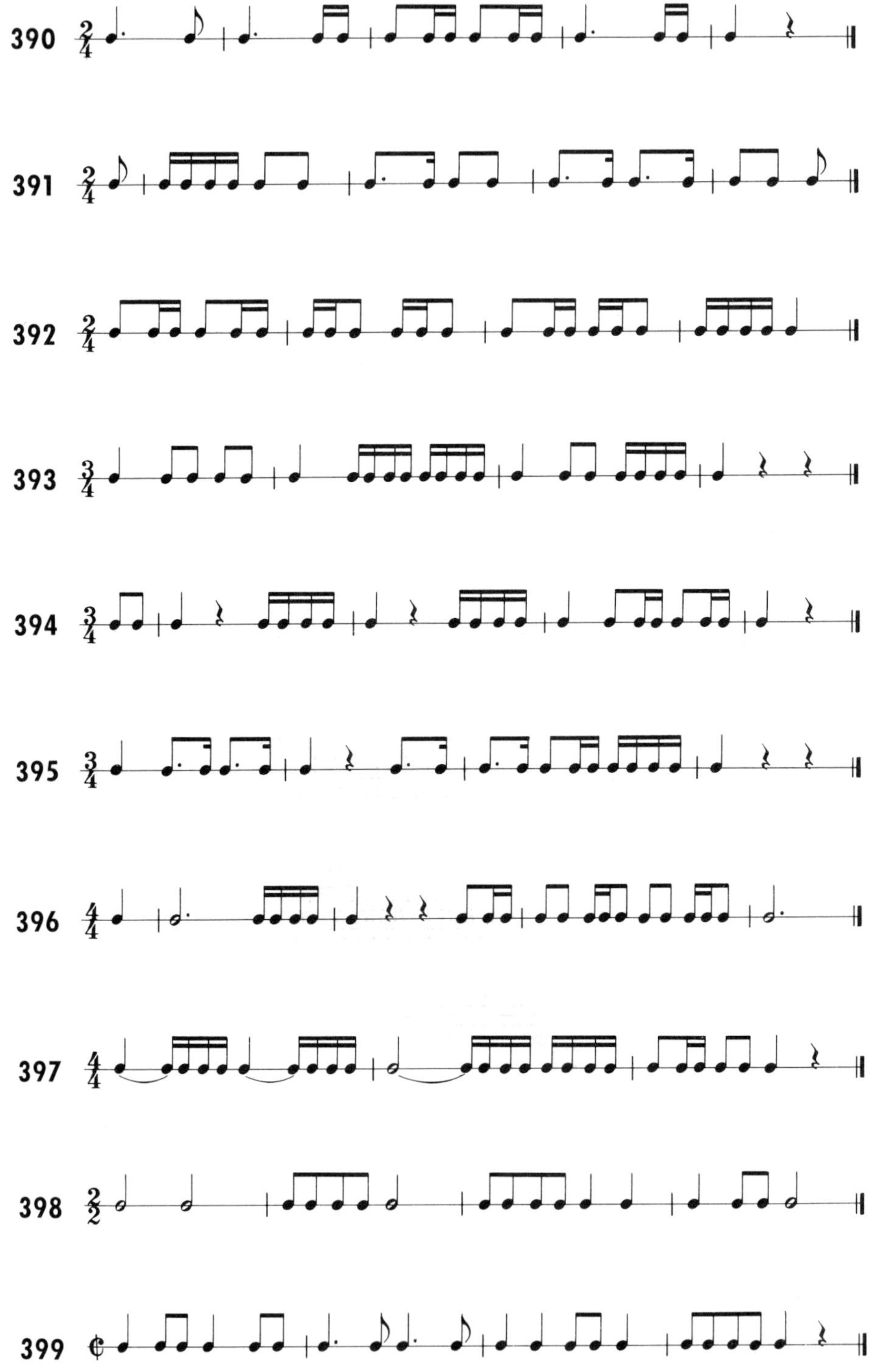
390
391
392
393
394
395
396
397
398
399

COMPOUND TIME

In compound time, the beat may be subdivided into six parts—for example, 6/8 ♩. = ♬♬♬ , 6/4 𝅗𝅥. = ♫ ♫ ♫ , 6/16 ♪. = ♬♬♬ , and so forth.

Rhythmic syllables may be used as follows:

(a) All note values shorter than the beat may be read using the syllable "ta."

(b) When using "la lee" for beat divisions, note values shorter than the beat division are read using the syllable "ta."

Section 3. Preliminary exercises, compound time.

Follow directions for similar exercises in simple time, page 104.

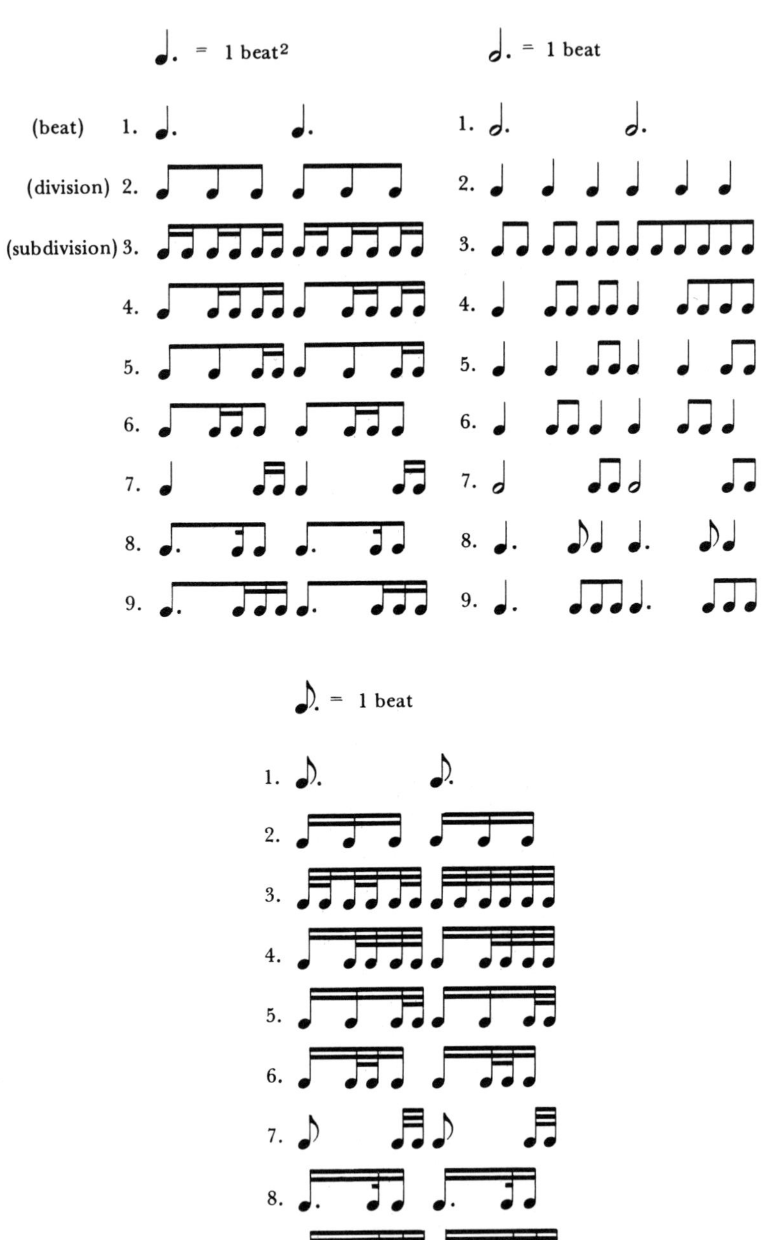

[2]These patterns are the most common of those possible.

Section 4. Rhythmic reading exercises in compound time.

Section 5. Two-part drills, simple time.

422
423
424
425
426
427
428
429

Section 6. Two-part drills, compound time.

♩. = 1 beat
437
♩. = 1 beat
438

CHAPTER 9

MELODY
further use of diatonic intervals

RHYTHM
the subdivided beat in simple and compound time

Section 1. Intervals from the tonic and dominant triads.

439

440

Allegretto
441
France
f
mf
f
Fine
f repeat p
D.C. al Fine
Tres vif
442
France
mf
Animé
443
France
f
mf
f
Canon for 5 voices
444
Praetorius
1
2
3
4
5

445
Allegro
Finland
446
Andante
Ohio
447
Con moto
Texas
448
Canon for 3 voices
Beethoven

Langsam
Schubert, Die Leiermann, Op. 89, No. 24
449
pp
Slow
Mexico
450
mp
Allegro non troppo
Italy
451
p
mp
f
mp
p
Allegro
Russia
452
f
Andantino
Italy
453
mf

cresc.
dim.
p
Andante
England
454
mp
mf
Andante
Scotland
455
mf
cresc.
f
England
Gaily
456
f

Section 2. The minor third between the second and fourth scale degrees (review Chapter 7, Section 1).

mf
p
cresc.
rit
f a tempo

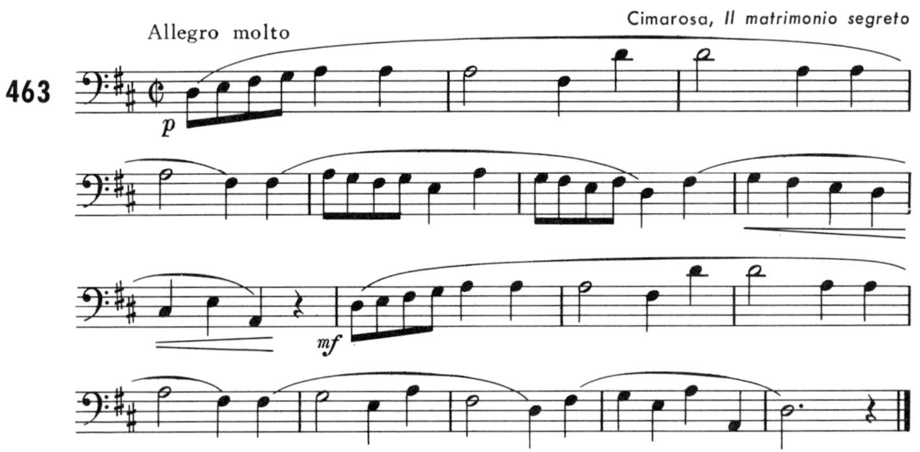

Allegro molto
Cimarosa, Il matrimonio segreto
463
p
mf

Vigorously
Finland
464
f
mf
f

Canon for 4 voices
Haydn
465
1
2
3
4

466
Allegro
Silesia
f
467
Moderato
Schubert, Klage an den Mond
p
cresc.
468
♩.=92
England
mf
mp
f
mp
p
469
Con moto
Gounod, Dites, la jeune belle
p
470
Larghetto
Germany
mp

Fine
D.C.

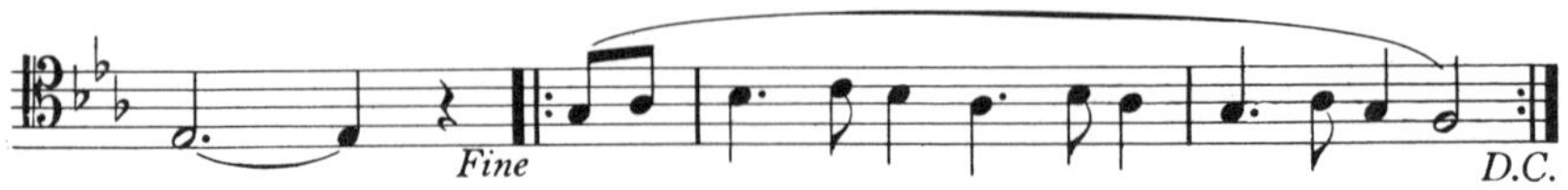

Section 3. Triad implication (review Chapter 7, Section 2).

Lively — Germany

471

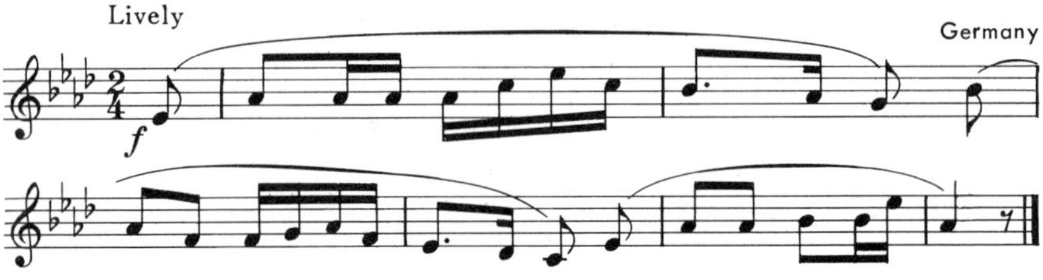
f

Moderato — France

472

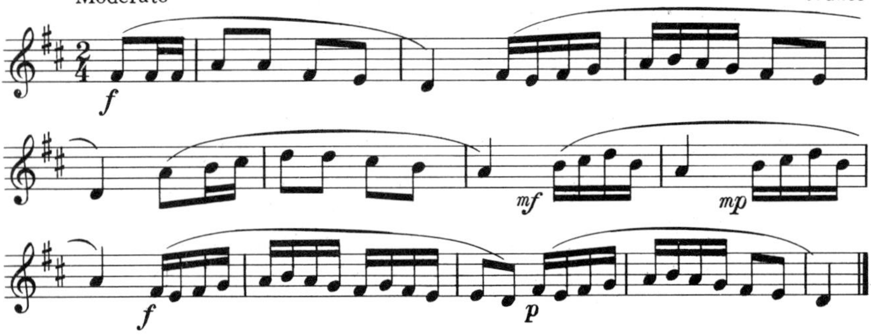
f
mf
mp
f
p

Adagio — France

473

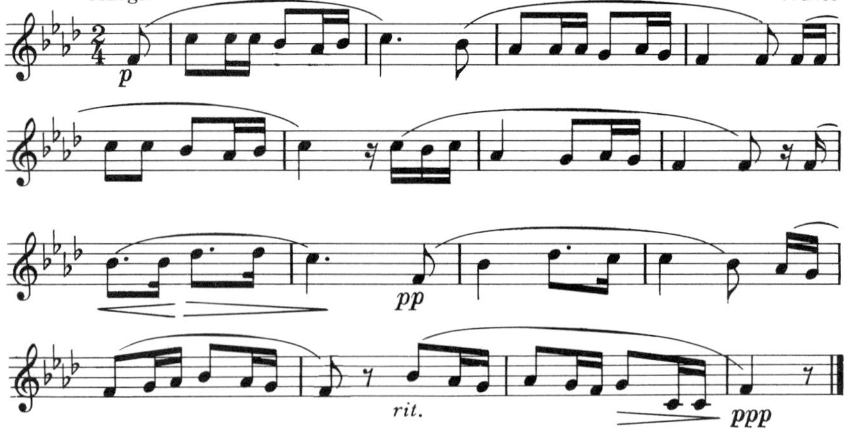
p
pp
rit.
ppp

474
Alla marcia
Germany
f
marcato
475
Allegretto
Alabama
mf
476
Allegro
Mozart, Quartet No. 17, K. 458
p
f
p
f
477
Allegro
France
mp
Fine
D.C. al Fine

Con moto — Germany (Brahms)

478

Allegro — Mozart, *The Magic Flute*, K. 620

479

Allegretto — Sweden

480

Moderato
Argentina
481
mp
cresc.
mf
Canon for 3 voices
Schubert
482
1
2
3
Moderato
Germany
483
p
Slowly
Alabama
484
p

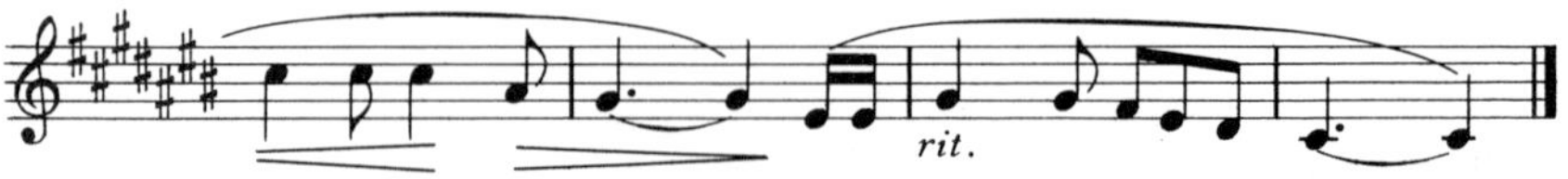

rit.

♩. = 1 beat

Costa Rica

485

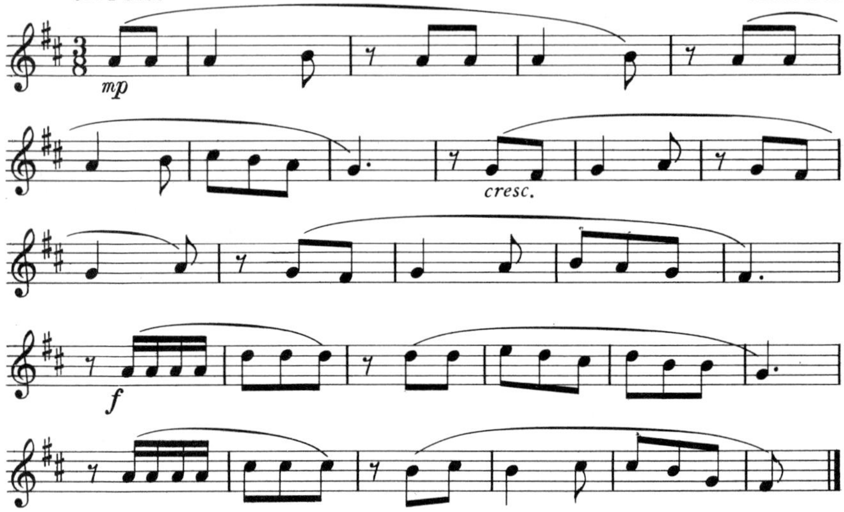

mp

cresc.

f

Section 4. Other intervallic implications (review Chapter 7, Section 3).

Allegro con brio
Haydn, Quartet, Op. 64, No.4
488
p
sf
Allegro
Mozart, Horn Quartet, K. 407
489
p
Andante
Sweden
490
p
Fine
D.C.
Allegretto
Grieg, Lauf der Welt
491
pp
rit.
a tempo

Teneramente
Stephen Foster, The Village Maiden
492
mp
mf

Canon for 3 voices
J. Hilton (17th century)
493
1
2
3

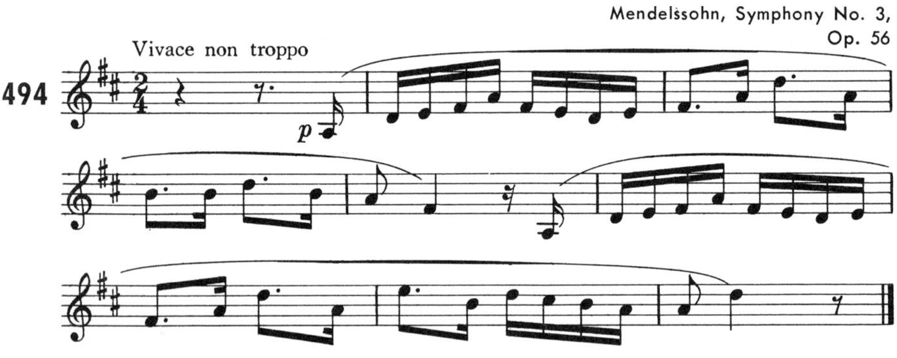
Mendelssohn, Symphony No. 3, Op. 56
Vivace non troppo
494
p

Rimsky-Korsakov, The Snow Maiden
Adagio
495
dolce

496
Allegretto
Grieg, Holberg Suite, Op. 40
pp
fpp
f
fz
Fine
f
D.C. al Fine
497
Canon for 3 voices
Samuel Arnold (1740–1802)
1
Haste thee nymph and bring with thee, jest and youth - ful
jol - li - ty,
2
Quips and cranks and wan - ton wiles,
nods and becks and wreath - ed smiles,
3
Sport that wrink - led
care de - rides, and laugh - ter hold - ing both his sides.
498
Andante
Mozart, Cosi fan tutte, K. 588
mp
p

Larghetto

Scotland

499

Couperin, *Soeur Monique*

Tendrement sans lenteur

500

Andante

Germany (Brahms)

501

502
Andante
Germany
mf
f
503
Allegro
Telemann, Tafel Musik
mf
p
mf
504
Allegro appassionato
Mendelssohn, Trio No. 2, Op. 66
mf
sf
mf
sf
505
Largo sostenuto
Haydn, Quartet, Op. 33, No. 2
p dolce

Bach, Motet, *Jesu, meine Freude*

506

Moderato

Russia

507

CHAPTER 10

MELODY

intervals from the dominant seventh (V^7) chord; other diatonic intervals of the seventh

RHYTHM

the divided beat and the subdivided beat; simple and compound time

Of all the possible intervals from the V^7 chord, only intervals of the third have been presented previously. The others are:

Chord members 1 up to 7 or 7 down to 1 = minor seventh (m7)
Chord members 3 up to 7 or 7 down to 3 = diminished fifth (d5), or tritone[1]
Chord members 7 up to 3 or 3 down to 7 = augmented fourth (A4), or tritone

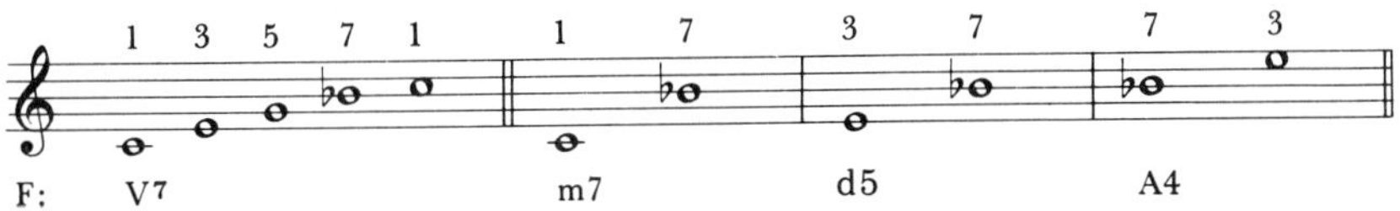

Section 1. The complete dominant seventh chord.

In this section, successive chord tones outline a complete four-note V^7 chord or a near-complete V^7 chord (1–5–7 or 3–5–7, or the reverse), all utilizing only intervals of the third and fifth.

[1]Each of the intervals produced by chord members 3 and 7 is also known as a *tritone;* each encompasses the equivalent of three whole steps.

a) The divided beat.

Allegro
Ireland
513

Andante ♩. = 58
Fauré, Les Berceaux
514
cresc.

Allegro
Germany
515

b) The subdivided beat.

Section 2. The interval of the minor seventh: chord members 1 up to 7 or reverse.

a) The divided beat.

Allegretto
England
524
f
mf
f

Animé
France
525
mf
Fine
f
D.C.

Andante
Germany
526
p
mp

Haydn, Divertimento
527
Fine
D.C.
Allegro
France
528
mf
Fine
f
D.C.
♩. = 1 beat
Mexico
529
f
ff
f
mf

b) The subdivided beat.

Handel, *Judas Maccabaeus*

534

Marcello (1686–1739), Cantata,
L'usignolo che il suo duolo

535

Adagio

mf

p

cresc.

f

Section 3. The interval of the tritone.

a) The divided beat.

mf
mf
Moderato ma con moto
Poland
540
mf
p
mf
sfz
sfz
sfz
f
Mutig
Germany
541
f
mf
f
Allegro con spirito
Sweden
542
mf
p

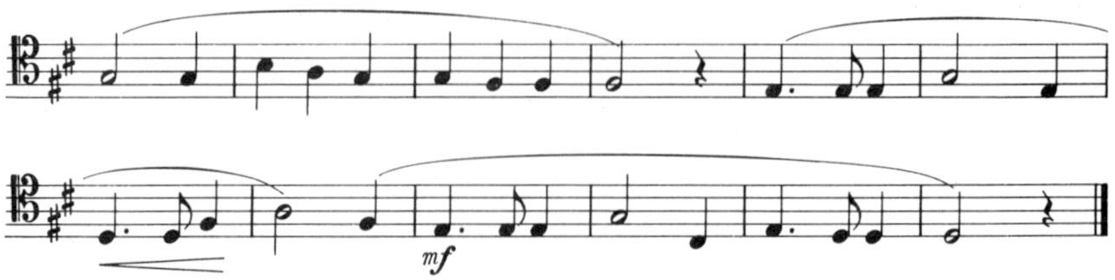
mf

Schumann, *Blondels Lied*, Op. 53, No. 1

Nicht schnell

543

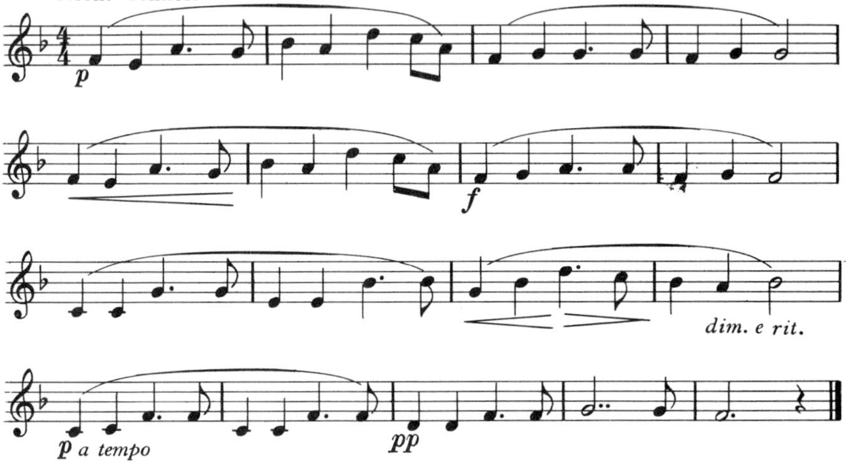
p
f
dim. e rit.
p a tempo
pp

b) The subdivided beat.

Allegretto

Germany

544

mf
mf
f

Canon for 3 voices

Salieri (1759–1825)

545

1

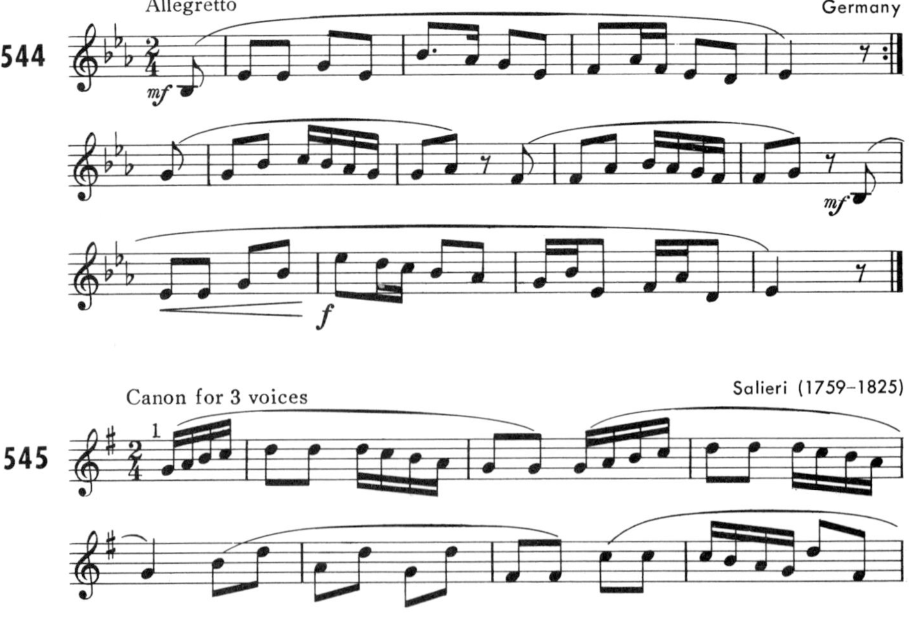

2

3

546 Allegro — Germany

mp *mf*

f

547 Allegro — Martinique

1.

2.

548 Andante — Arlberg (1830-1896), *Svärmeri*

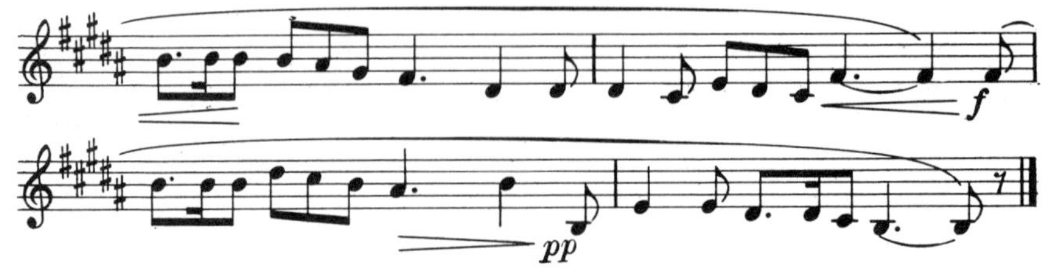

Section 4. Other diatonic intervals of the seventh.

Mozart, Quartet, K. 428

Allegretto

549

f

Lightly

England

550

mf

p *cresc.*

mf

cresc.

mf

Allegro

Haydn, Piano Sonata in E♭ major(1780)

551

f

Allegro

Haydn, Piano Sonata in C major(1791)

552

p

553
♩. = 1 beat
Louisiana
mf
f
554
Canon for 3 voices
Purcell
1
2
3
555
Hindemith, Let's Build a Town
556
Andante cantabile
Schumann, Piano Quartet, Op. 47
p

Rachmaninoff, Symphony No.2

557

Bach, *Well Tembered Clavier,* Vol. I, Fugue 15

558

Section 5. Duets.

Mozart, *Marriage of Figaro,* K.492

559

Allegro vivace (𝅗𝅥 = 1 beat)
Beethoven, Fidelio, Op.72
560
Allegro ma non troppo
Germany
561
*
mp
mp
f
f
mp
mp

Allegretto e marcato

Germany

562

*

Allegro

Vivaldi, Trio Sonata, Op. 1, No. 2

563

CHAPTER 11

MELODY:

Chromaticism (I)[1]

chromatic nonharmonic tones; the dominant of the dominant (V/V) harmony; modulation from a major key to its dominant

Section 1. Chromatic nonharmonic tones.

[1]The study of chromaticism in sight singing includes chromatically altered tones, implied secondary dominant and altered harmonies, and modulation. Materials not presented in this chapter will be found in Chapters 12 and 19.

Andante
Canada
566
f
f
p
Andante
Schubert, Mass in E♭
567
Zartlich
J. Ruprech, An Röschen (1785)
568
Allegro assai
Haydn, Farewell Symphony
569
pp

570
Moderato
Costa Rica
mp
cresc.
mf
p
571
Mozart, Minuet, K.164
572
Con moto
Schubert, Frühlingstraum, Op. 89, No 11
p
mp
573
Allegretto
Joseph Steffan (1726–1797), Gold'ne Freiheit
mf
rit.
mf
f

Section 2. The secondary dominant chord, V/V or V^7/V; modulation from a major key to its dominant.

The secondary dominant progression V/V–V (in C, D F♯ A–G B D) can be found within a phrase or at a cadence point. At a cadence, its aural impression can range from a half cadence on the dominant to a full modulation to the key of the dominant. Melodies 578–581 illustrate some of these possibilities.

Melody 578: In F major, the B♮ implies the progression G B D (V/V) to C E G B♭ (V^7) within the phrase.

Melody 579: In D major, the G♯ at the cadence, measure 7, produces an effect of V–I (E G♯ B–A C♯ E) in A major, but so temporary as to be best considered as V/V–V in D major.

Melody 580: The occurrence of the V/V–V progression at measures 7–8 produces a stronger but not a positive impression of A major.

Melody 581: In this C major melody, the impression of modulation to G major is emphasized by several repetitions of V–I in G major and by the final arpeggiation of the G major triad.

After number 581, the melodies may imply any of these interpretations. Often two interpretations of the same passage may be equally valid, depending upon the subjective impression upon the listener.

Observe that any progression described above can occur without an accidental in the melodic line. When not present in the given line, the accidental is implied or occurs in another voice. See, for example, melody 580, measures 11–12, progression I V/V V,
DF♯ A E G♯ B A C♯ E
where only B of the V/V harmony is seen. Melody 585 includes no accidental, but one of its cadences can easily be considered a secondary dominant progression. Similar examples will be found in modulating melodies from later chapters.

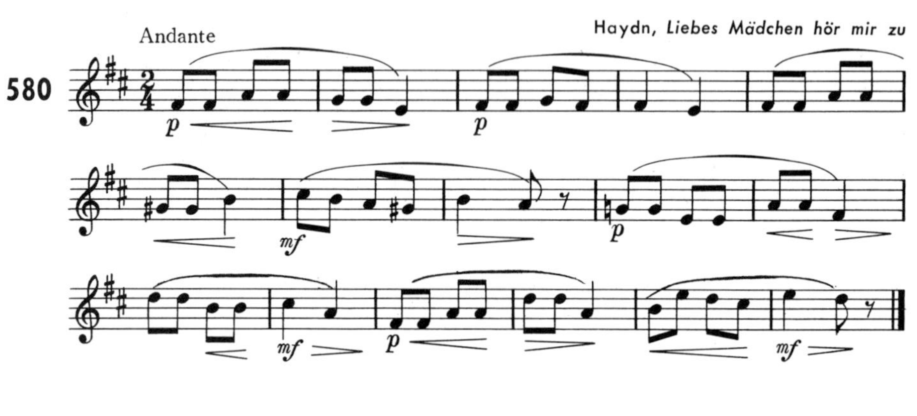

*In addition to its usual upward resolution, a secondary leading tone often resolves down by chromatic half step to the seventh of a dominant seventh or a secondary dominant seventh chord.

Brahms, *Vergebliches Ständchen,* Op. 84, No. 4
Animated
584
f
p
pp

Germany (Brahms)
Allegro
585
mf

Orlando Gibbons, Psalm 21
=92
586

Purcell, The Fairy Queen
Andante
587
mp
1.
2.
Mendelssohn, Morgenlied, Op. 86, No. 2
Allegro vivace
588
p
f
Allegro
Swabia
589
f
Fine
mf
f
mf
f rit.
D.C. al Fine

Allegro
Mozart, Sehnsuch nach dem Frühlinge, K. 596
590

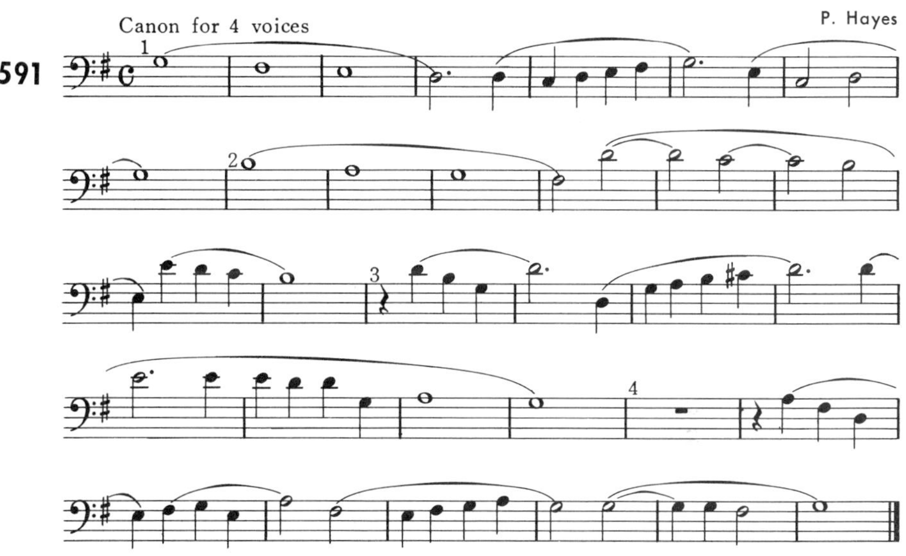
Canon for 4 voices
P. Hayes
591
1
2
3
4

Munter
Schumann, Der Zeizig, Op. 104, No. 4
592
p
f

Schubert, *Der Alpenjäger*, Op. 13, No. 3
Frisch
593
mf
f
mf
f
f
Beethoven, *Busslied*, Op. 48, No. 5
Allegro
594
p
cresc.
p
Schumann, *Du Ring am meinem Finger*, Op. 42, No. 4
Innig
595
p

Allegretto vivace
Mozart, Cosi fan tutte, K. 588
596
p
Fine
D.C.
Nicht schnell
Schumann, Marienwürmchen, Op. 79, No. 14
597
p
fp

Larghetto
Mozart, Clarinet Quintet, K. 581
598
Grave
J. Peri (c. 1600), Orfeo
599
Allegro
Mozart, Divertimento, K. 131
600

Schubert, Mit dem grünen Lautenbande
Moderato
601
p
rit.
p
rit.
Nörmiger's Tablaturbuch (1598)
Largo
602
mp
cresc.
f
mp
Allegro
Germany
603
mf

Andante
Arriaga (1822), Quartet No. 2
604
p
mf
dim. e rit.
p a tempo
Schumann, Der Kartenlegerin, Op. 31, No 2
Allegro
605
p
rit.
a tempo
Pasquini (1637–1710), Quanto è folle
Andantino
606
p
mf
dim.
p
mp
mf

Allegro
Beethoven, Quartet No. 12, Op. 127
607
p
1.
2.
Vivace
Telemann, Die Ehre des Herrlichen
608
f
p
f
p
cresc.
f
mp
cresc.
f
Allegretto
Handel, Xerxes
609
mp
mp

Allegretto
Mozart, Zufriedenheit
610
p
mp
cresc.
f
dim.
mp
Allegro ma non troppo
Mozart, Quartet, K. 421
611
p
Larghetto
Mozart, Ridente la calma, K. 152
612
p

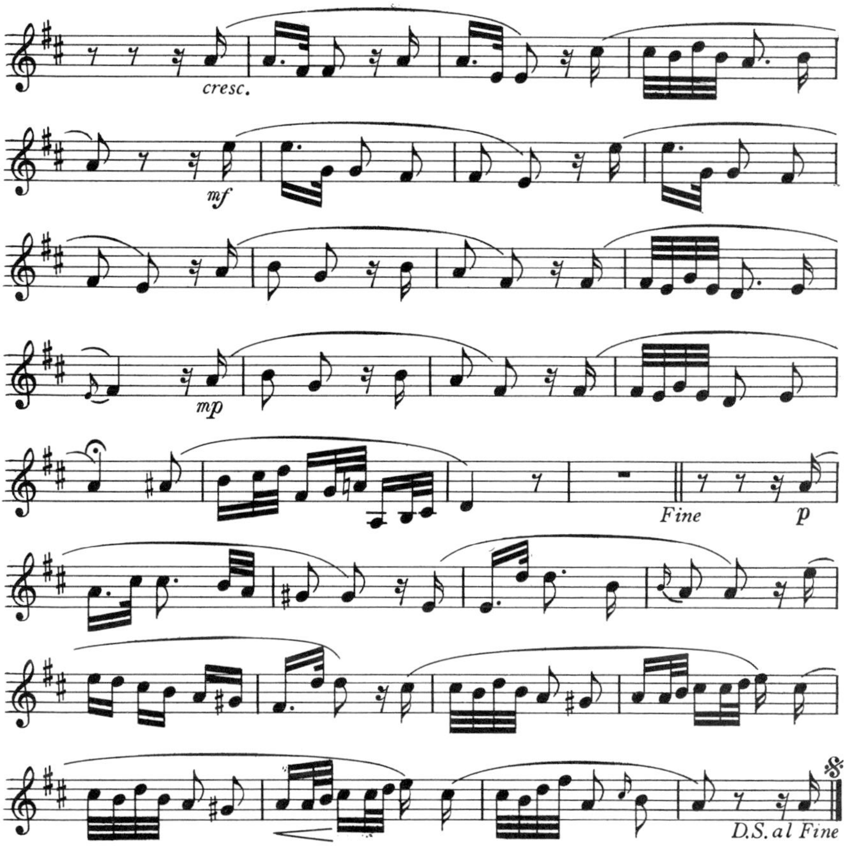
cresc.
mf
mp
Fine
p
D.S. al Fine

Section 3. Duets.

Allegretto

Germany

613

p
p
cresc.
cresc.
mf
mf
p
p

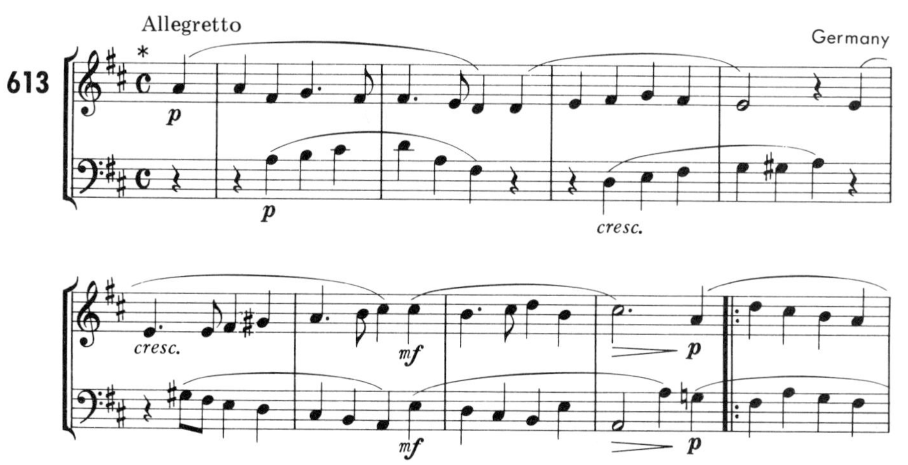

1.
2.

Moderato — Germany

614

*
mf
Fine
mp
mp
D.C.

Allegro — Germany

615

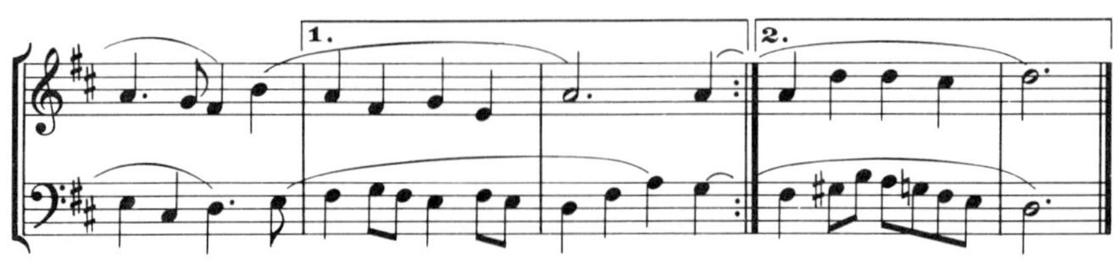

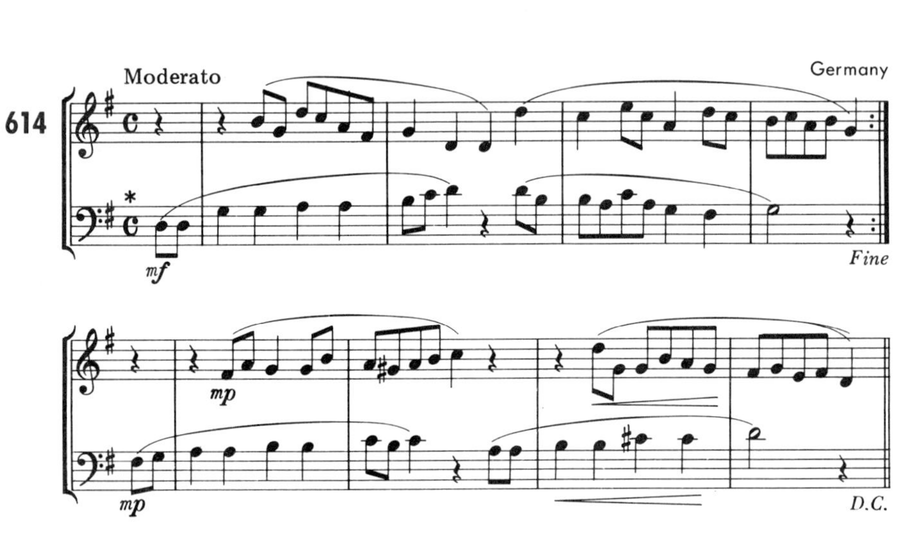

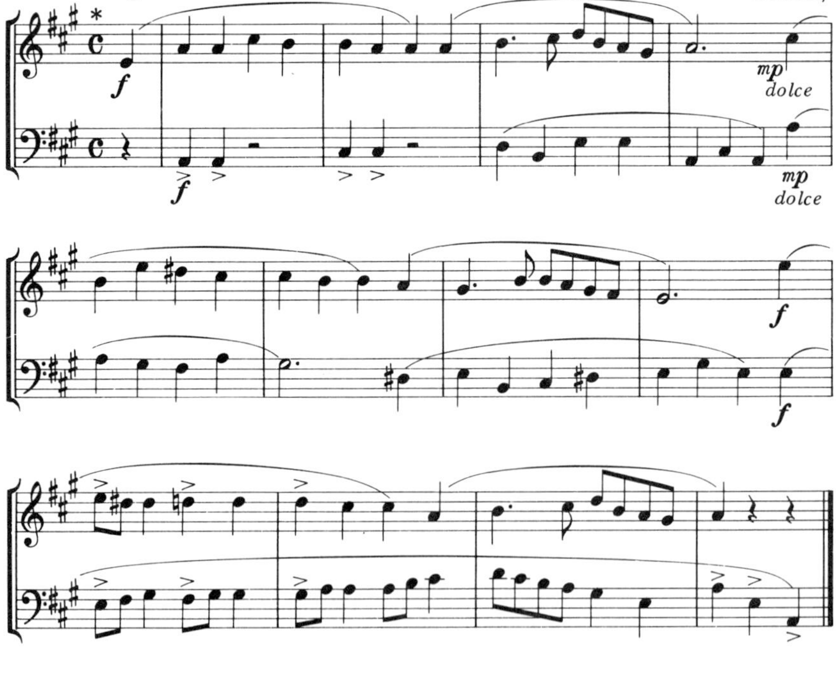
*
f
f
mp
dolce
mp
dolce
f
f

Mozart, The Magic Flute, K. 620
Larghetto
616
p
p
f
f
Mozart, Quartet, K. 575
Allegretto
617
p
p
Stamitz, Concerto für Basset Horn
Allegro
618

Andante
Mozart, Symphony No. 35, Prague, K. 504
619
p
Allegro
Berlioz, The Damnation of Faust
620
mf
mf
1.
2.

CHAPTER 12

MELODY:
Chromaticism (II); secondary dominant harmony, other than V/V; modulation to closely related keys, continued

Section 1. Secondary dominant chords other than V/V.

Any major or minor triad may be preceded by its secondary dominant chord, often implied by a chromatically altered tone.[1] In melody 621, for example, the F♯ in measure 3 represents V/ii in the progression V/ii–ii (D F♯A–G B♭ D). In addition to chromatically raised tones, an occasional lowered tone will imply a secondary dominant chord, as in the V^7/IV where, in C major, the tone B♭ may imply C E G B♭, the V^7/IV.

As discussed in the previous chapter, subjective evaluation of this type of progression may indicate modulation, or similarly, in Section 2 following, some examples of modulation could be considered simply as secondary dominant progressions.

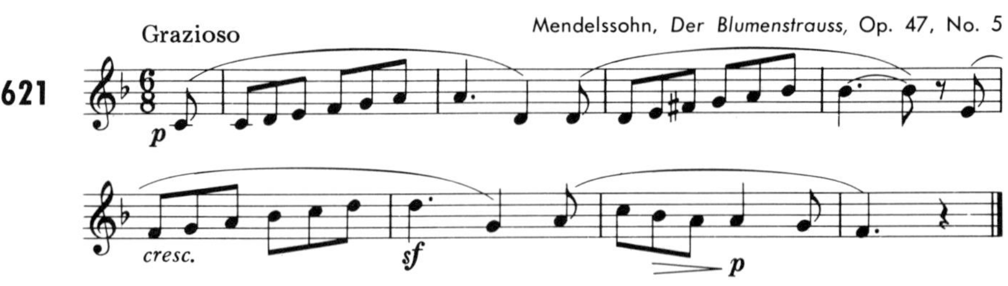

[1]Again, the diatonic tones of a chord may also imply a secondary function. Review page 155, discussion of melody 580.

Giocoso
Virgin Islands
622
mp
mf
1.
2.
Canon for 3 voices
Beethoven
623
1
2
3
Canon for 4 voices
Germany
624
1
2
3
4
Allegro
Schubert, An den Frühling
625
p

cresc.
p

Andantino
Berlioz, The Damnation of Faust
626
p

Germany
Allegro
627
mf
f
ff
mf

Mozart, La Clemenza di Tito, K. 621
Andante
628
p

Brahms, *Geliebter, wo zaudert,* Op. 33, No. 13

629 

Beethoven

630 Canon for 3 voices

Haydn, Quartet, Op. 71, No. 3

631 Andante con moto

Section 2. Modulations from a major key to closely related keys other than the dominant.[2]

We have seen that it is often difficult to determine whether a progression is a modulation to the key of the dominant or a half cadence in the original key. Any modulation to a key other than to the dominant from a major key is more convincing since its cadence usually has little if any inclination to return immediately to the original key.

Of all possible modulations to closely related keys, those to the dominant from a major key and to the relative major (to the mediant) from a minor key are by far the most common. Note that from a minor key, modulation to the dominant is to a *minor* key, for example, C minor to G *minor.*

[2]When the signatures of two keys are the same, or differ by not more than one sharp or one flat, the keys are *closely* related. Examples:

from C major to D minor (1♭)	from C minor to E♭ major (3♭)
E minor (1♯)	F minor (4♭)
F major (1♭)	G minor (2♭)
G major (1♯)	A♭ major (4♭)
A minor (0♯ or ♭)	B♭ major (2♭)

mf

Allegro
Fauré, *Fleur Jetée*
634
f
mf
f

Andante
Beethoven, *Sehnsucht*, Op. 83, No. 2
635
mp
cresc.
mp
cresc.
rit
a tempo

Presto
Beethoven, Quartet No. 13, Op. 130
636
pp

cresc.
f
Andante con moto
Schubert, Rosamunde, Op. 26
637
p
Mendelssohn, Romanze, Op. 8, No. 11
Andante
638
p
Langsam
Germany (Brahms)
639
p

640
Canon for 3 voices
Purcell
1
2
3
641
Canon for 2 voices
Haydn, Quartet, Op. 76, No. 2
1
2

642
Allegro
Purcell, King Arthur
f
Fine
D.S. al Fine

643
Langsam
Schubert, Das Zügenlächlein
p
cresc.
f

644
Andante
Liszt, Angiolin dal biondo crin
pp dolce
poco rit.
a tempo
poco rit.

645
Allegretto
Italy
f
p

mp
Presto
Haydn, Piano Sonata (1776)
646
Allegro moderato
Purcell, Dido and Aeneas
647
f
p
f
p
f
Fine
mp
cresc.
f
D.S. al Fine
♩. = 1 beat
Spain
648
mf

Canon for 3 voices
Cranford (17th century)
649
1
2
3
Allegro
Schumann, Quartet, Op. 41, No. 3
650
p
Andante con moto
Mendelssohn, Jagdlied, Op. 84, No. 3
651
mf
f
mf
f

p

Gracieusement

Rameau, *Hippolyte et Aricie*

652

p

Canon for 3 voices

Couperin

653

654
Allegro
Mozart, Quintet, K. 406
p
655
Andantino
Franz, Mutter, o sing mich zur Ruh!
p
mf
p
mf
656
Mit innigkeit
Germany
p
mf
pp
657
Andantino
Germany
p

p
Lento
France
658
p
p
mp
p
pp
Ziemlich langsam
Schumann, *Myrten,* Op. 25
659
p
rit.
rit.
p
p
rit.
pp
rit.
Andante
Durante (1684-1755), *Vergin Tutto Amor*
660

Allegro molto
Beethoven, Quartet No. 2, Op. 18, No. 2
661
p
cresc.
f
sf
sf
Allegro
Mendelssohn, Italien, Op. 8 No. 3
662
p
f
p

Schumann, *Schlusslied des Narren*, Op. 127, No. 5

Allegro

663

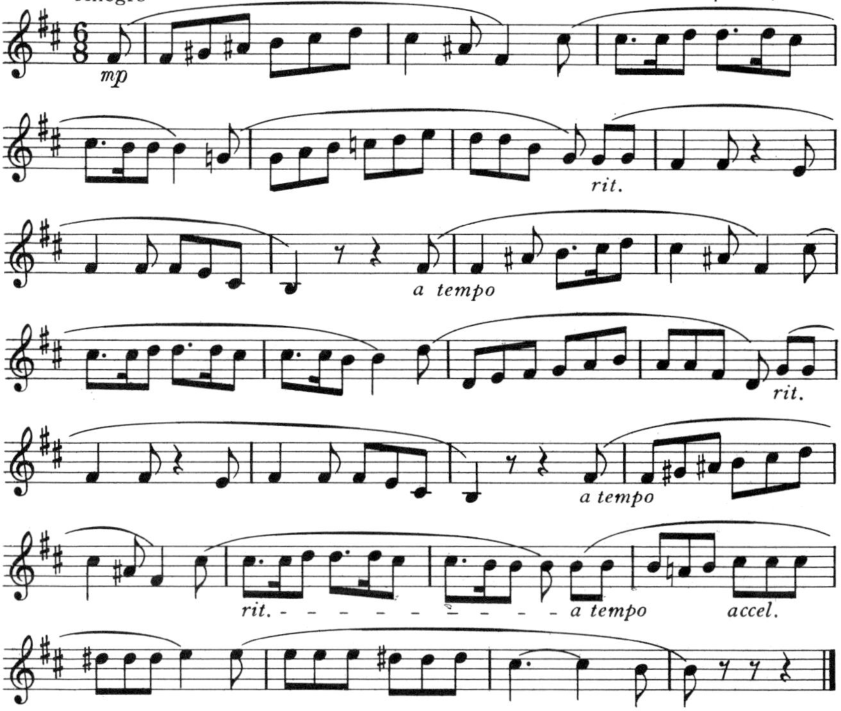
mp
rit.
a tempo
rit.
a tempo
rit. - - - - - - - - - - - - a tempo
accel.

Section 3. Duets.

Included are examples of both secondary dominant progressions and modulations to closely related keys.

Haydn, Quartet, Op. 33, No. 6

Allegro

664

mf

Haydn, *The Creation*

Allegro

665

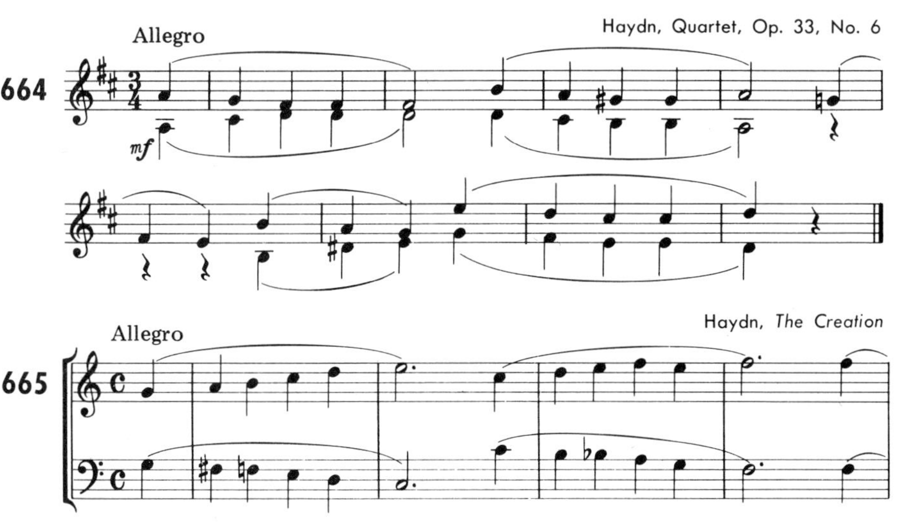

666

Allegro

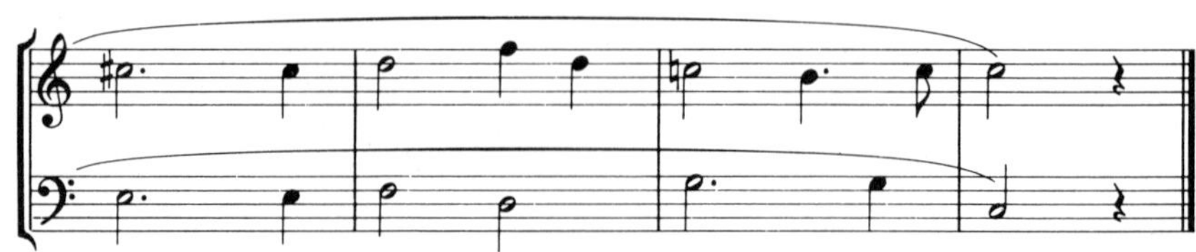

Mozart, *The Magic Flute*, K. 620

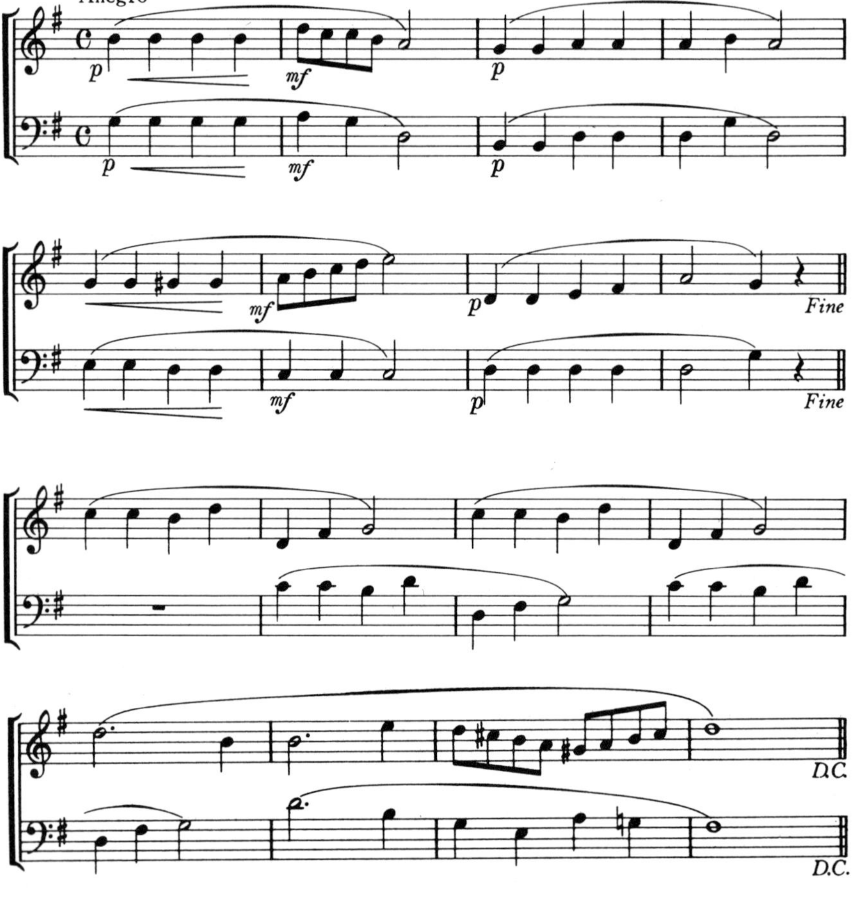
p
mf
p
p
mf
p
mf
p
Fine
mf
p
Fine
D.C.
D.C.

667

Tenderly

Schumann, *Schön Blümelein*, Op. 43, No. 3

p

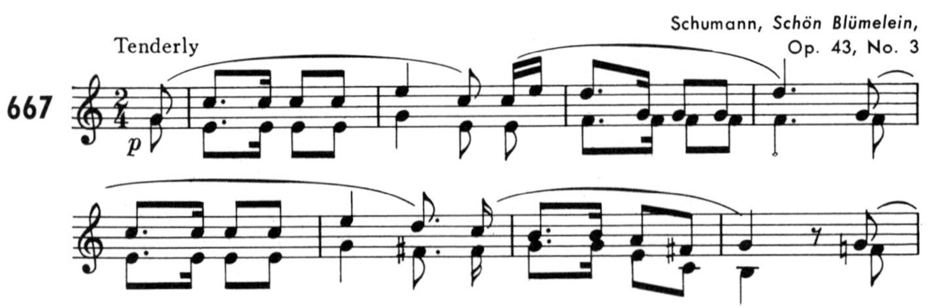

rit.
Moderato
Beethoven, Fidelio, Op. 72
668
p
p
Allegro con brio
Brahms, Piano Trio, Op. 8
669
p
cresc.

poco f
poco f
cresc.
cresc.
Allegro ma non troppo
Mozart, Quartet, K. 464
670
p
Andante
Gluck, Iphigenie auf Tauris
671
p
mf
mp
p

Sances (1600-1659), *Chi nel Regno*

672

Handel, *Julius Caesar*

673

Dittersdorf, Doktor und Apotheker
Vivace
674
Couperin, Les Moisonneurs
675
Brahms, Liebeslieder Walzer, Op. 52
Im Ländler tempo
676

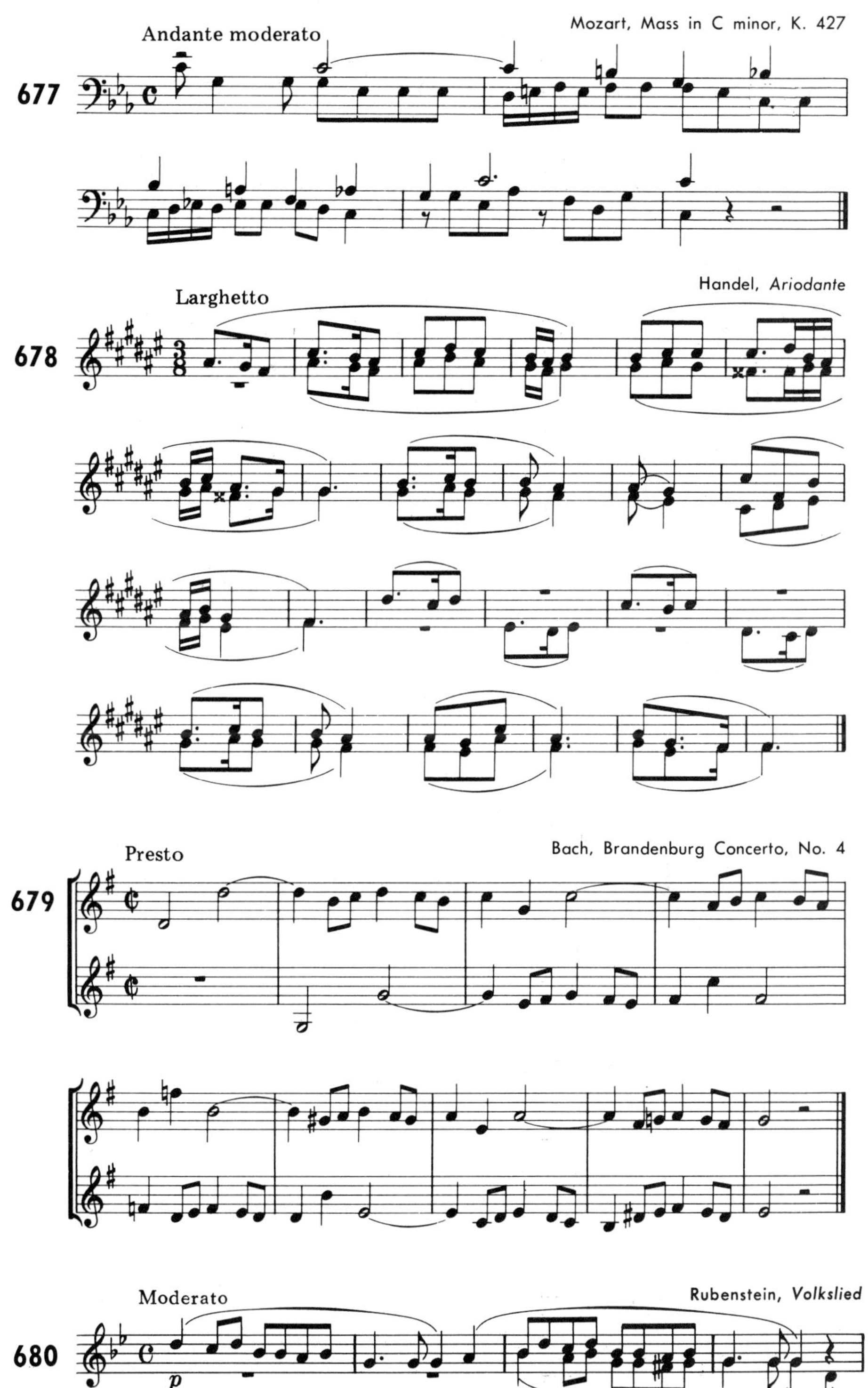
Andante moderato
Mozart, Mass in C minor, K. 427
677
Larghetto
Handel, *Ariodante*
678
Presto
Bach, Brandenburg Concerto, No. 4
679
Moderato
Rubenstein, *Volkslied*
680
p

cresc.
cresc.
dim.
cresc.
dim.
p
Adagio
Corelli, Sonata da Chiesa, Op. 3, No. 2
681

682
Largo
Handel, *Julius Caesar*
683
Allegro
Vivaldi, Trio Sonata, Op. 1, No. 2

CHAPTER 13

RHYTHM

syncopation in beat-note and divided beat patterns

Syncopation occurs when the normal or expected pattern of meter or accent is deliberately upset. Syncopation can be created by

1. accenting a weak beat or a weak part of a beat:

2. tying a weak beat into the next strong beat:[1]

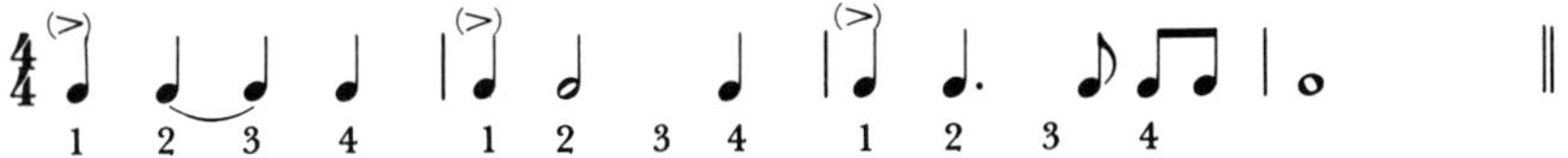

3. tying the weak part of a beat into the next beat:

[1]Some passages seemingly in syncopation may be subject to a different interpretation. For example, the pattern $\frac{3}{4}$ | | in some circumstances is performed as $\frac{3}{2}$ | |. See Chapter 17.

A. RHYTHMIC READING

Section 1. Syncopation, simple time.

694
695
696
697
698
699
Section 2. Syncopation, compound time.
700
701
702
703

704
705
706
707
708
709
710
Section 3. Two-part drills.
711
712
713

714
715
716
717
718
719
720

721

722
♩. = 1 beat

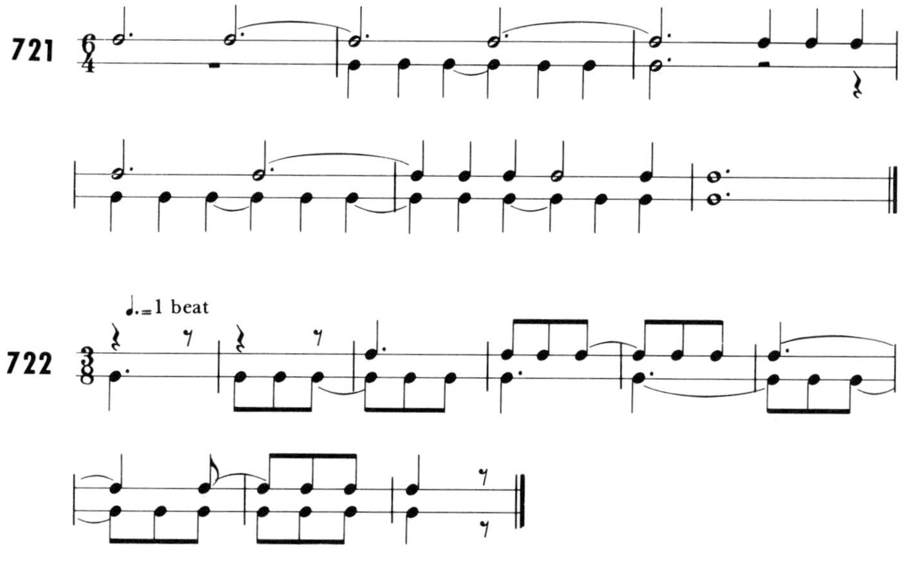

SIGHT SINGING, DIATONIC MELODIES

Section 4. Simple time.

723 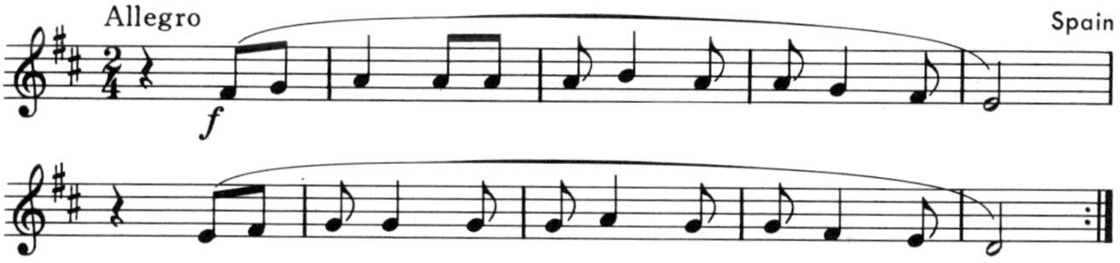
Allegro
Spain
f

724 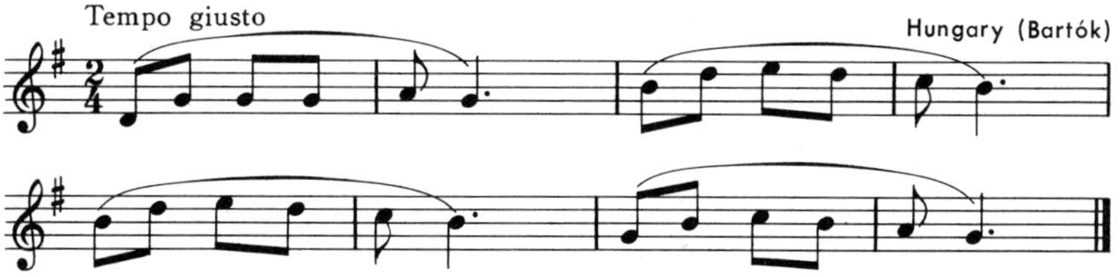
Tempo giusto
Hungary (Bartók)

725
Moderato commodo
Saint-Saëns, *Christmas Oratorio*
p

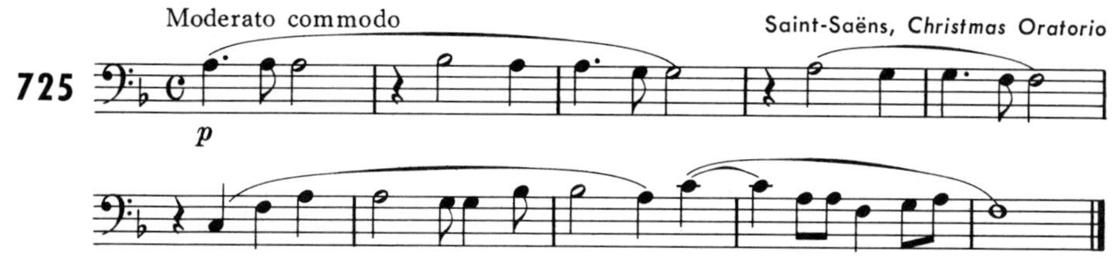

Brightly
Poland
726
mf
f
mf
mp
Allegro assai
Haydn, Divertimento
727
Tempo di menuetto
Mozart, Sonata No. 4 for Violin and Piano K. 304
728
Presto assai
Haydn, Symphony No. 47
729

730
Allegro 𝅗𝅥. = 36
Beethoven, Quartet No. 6, Op. 18, No. 6
p
sf
731
Andante
Spiritual, United States
mp
p
732
Canon for 3 voices
Caldara
1
2
3
733
Andante con moto
Bach, Motet, *Der Geist hilft unsrer Schwachheit auf*
mp

734

Allegro
Spain
f
mp
f

735

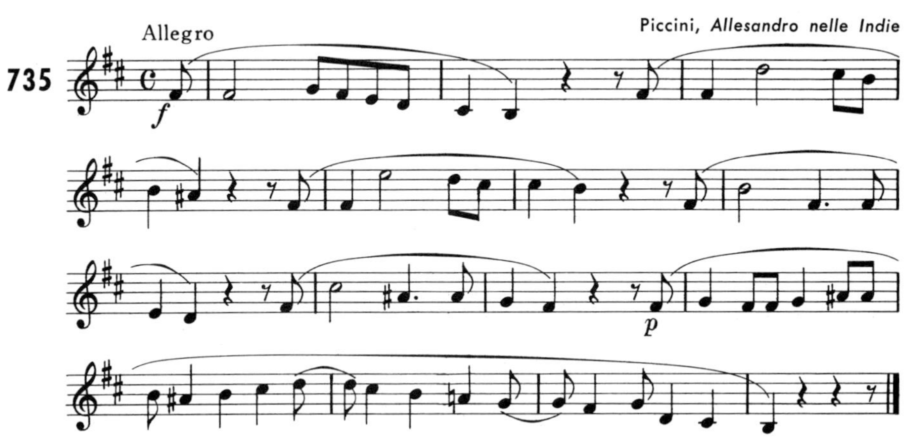
Allegro
Piccini, Allesandro nelle Indie
f
p

736

Allegretto
Dominican Republic
f

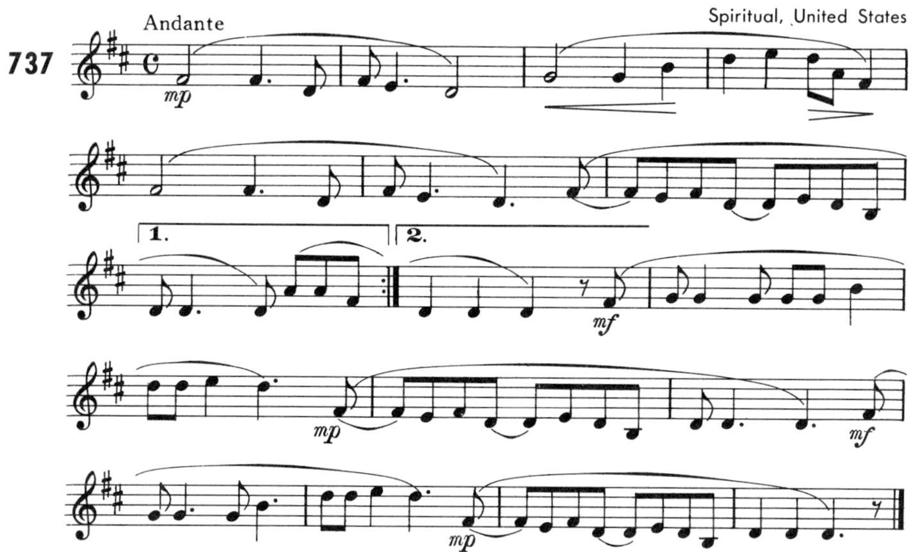

Spiritual, United States

737 Andante

mp
1.
2.
mf
mp
mf
mp

Beethoven, 'Cello Sonata No. 3, Op. 69

738 Allegro molto

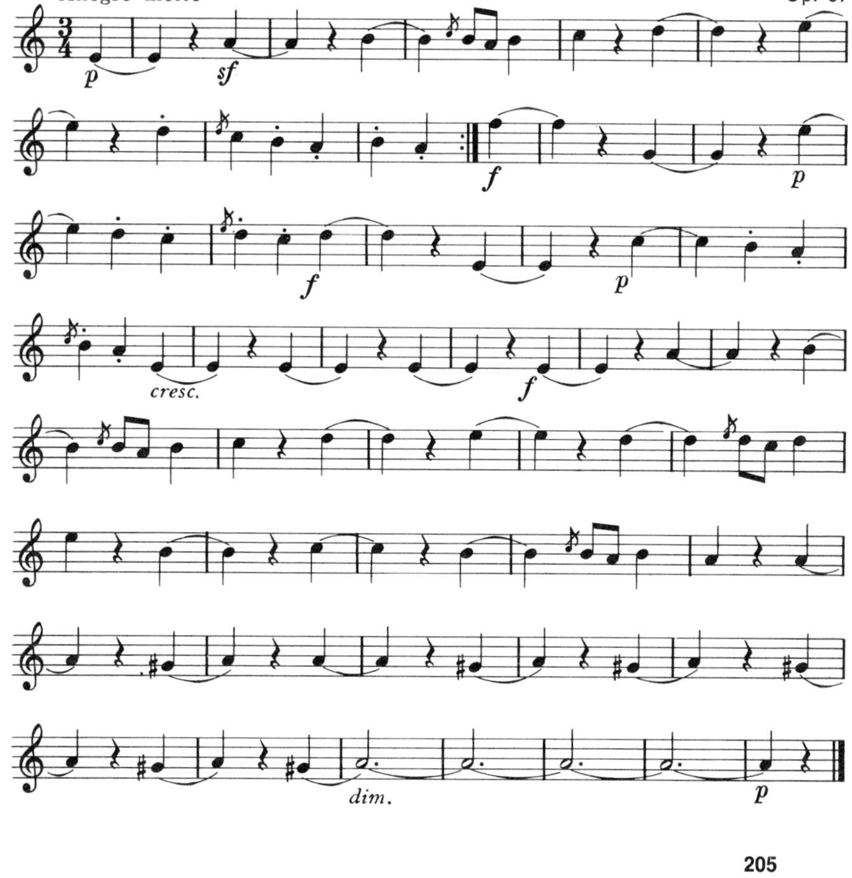

p
sf
f
p
f
p
cresc.
f
dim.
p

Section 5. Compound time.

The rhythmic figure in measure 1 of melody 739 looks like syncopation, but is usually performed with the accent on the strong beat: $\frac{6}{8}$ ♪ ♩ ♪ ♩ ‖. See Chapter 14 for other examples of this nature.

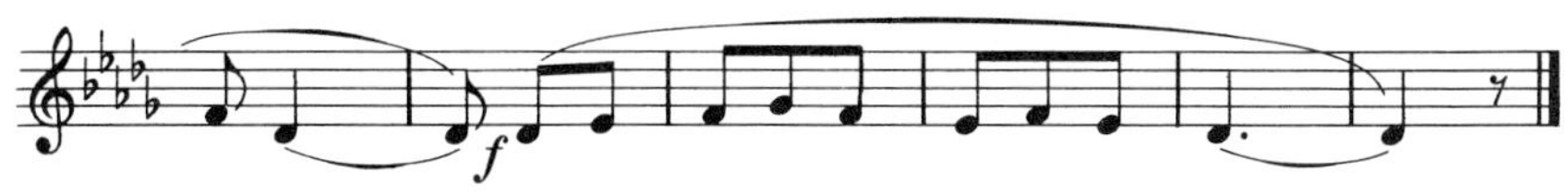

f

Cantabile

Arizona

742
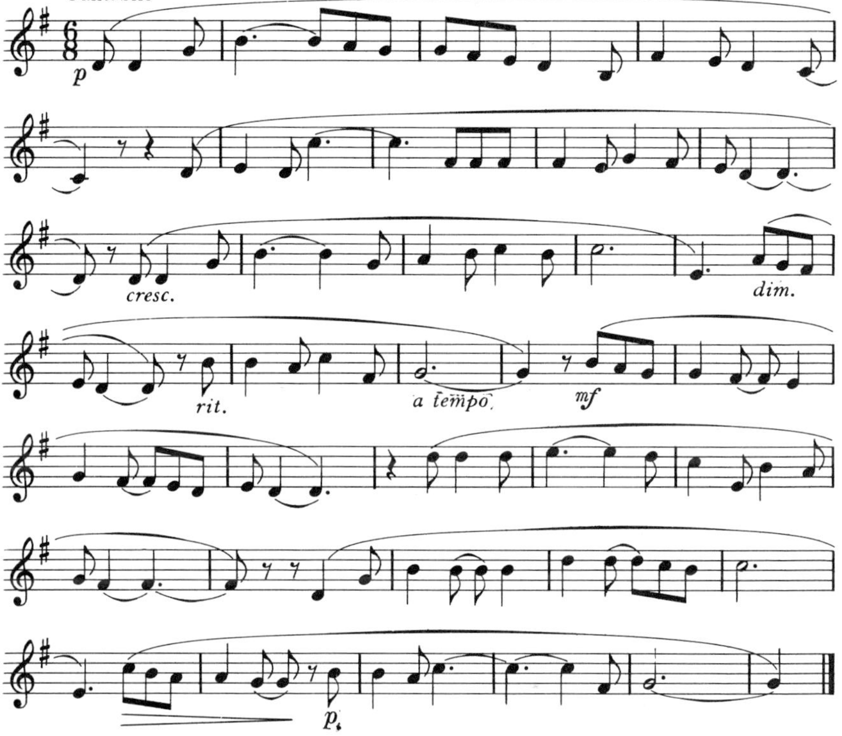
p
cresc.
dim.
rit.
a tempo
mf
p

Canon for 3 voices

England

743
1
2
3

Allegro

Mexico

744
f

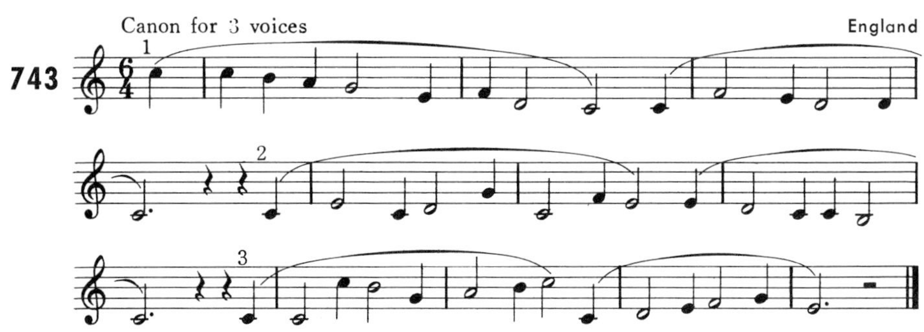

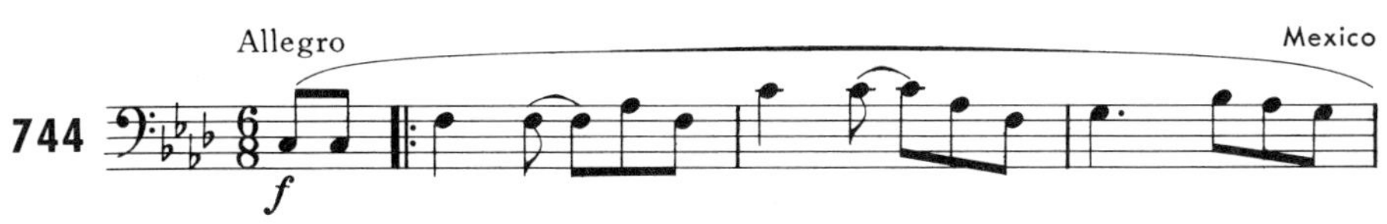

Section 6. Duets.

Allegretto
Bohemia
747
mf
mf
Fine
f
f
D.C.
Con spirito
Jamaica
748
mf
mf
f
f
decresc.
decresc.
mp
mp

749

750

Purcell, Dido and Aeneas
Fear no dan - ger to en - sue, the
repeat
Fear no dan - ger to en - sue, the
he - ro loves as well as you.
Fine
he - ro loves as well as you.
Fine
Ev - er gen tle, ev - er smil ing,
and the cares of life be guil ing
D.C.
D.C.
Andantino
Mozart, Luisita amabile, K. 480
dim.

fp
fp
dim.
dim.

CHAPTER 14

RHYTHM

syncopation in subdivided beat patterns

RHYTHMIC READING

Section 1. Single line drills.

756 $\frac{3}{4}$

757 $\frac{3}{4}$

758 $\frac{4}{4}$

759 $\frac{4}{4}$

760 C

761 $\frac{2}{2}$

762 C

763 $\frac{3}{2}$

764 $\frac{4}{2}$

765 $\frac{3}{8}$

766 $\frac{3}{8}$

767
768
769
Section 2. Two-part drills.
770
771
772
773
774

SIGHT SINGING

Section 3. Diatonic melodies.

(a) Melodies with subdivided beat patterns, but with syncopation only in divided beat patterns

Moderato — Haydn, Quartet, Op. 17, No. 1

777

f

p

Allegro — Muffat (1690–1770), Suite for Harpsichord

778

f

Assai agitato ♩. = 180 — Schumann, Quartet, Op. 41, No. 3

779

p

Loillet, Sonata for Flute, Op. 1, No. 1
Allegro
780
Vivardi, Concerto for Two Violins
Allegro
781
Telemann, Tafelmusik
Allegro
782

(b) Syncopation in subdivided beat patterns

783 Allegro — South Carolina

mp *mf*

784 Gaily — Louisiana

f

785 Allegretto — Scotland

mf *f* *mf*

786 Moderato — Florida

f

Allegro
Alabama
787
Allegretto
England
788
Allegro
Texas
789
Allegro
Spiritual, United States
790
Allegro
Spiritual, United States
791

Moderately fast
Spiritual, United States
792
mf
f
mf
f
mf
Moderato
Dominican Republic
793
f
Lento.
Georgia
794
p

Andante grazioso
Scotland
795
mf
mf
mp
Andante con moto
Panama
796
mf
f
p
mf
Allegro moderato
Brazil
797
mp
Con moto
Trinidad
798
p

Fine
f
D.C.
Andante
Puerto Rico
799
p
Giocoso
Haiti
800
f
Fine
mp
D.C.
Allegretto
West Indies Calypso*
801
mf
f
mf
mp

* By permission of copyright owner, M. Baron Co., New York. N. Y.

Section 4. Syncopation in chromatic melodies.

Loillet, Sonata for Flute, Op. 2, No. 3
Sarabande
805
Loillet, Sonata for Flute, Op. 2, No.3
Giga
806
Sarabande
Purcell, Suite V
807

Allegro
Pergolesi, Il Prigioniero superbo
808
Vivace assai
Haydn, Quartet, Op. 76, No. 2
809
p
Allegro con spirito
Haydn, Quartet, Op. 64, No. 3
810
mf

Section 5. Duets.

♩. = 1 beat

Spain

812

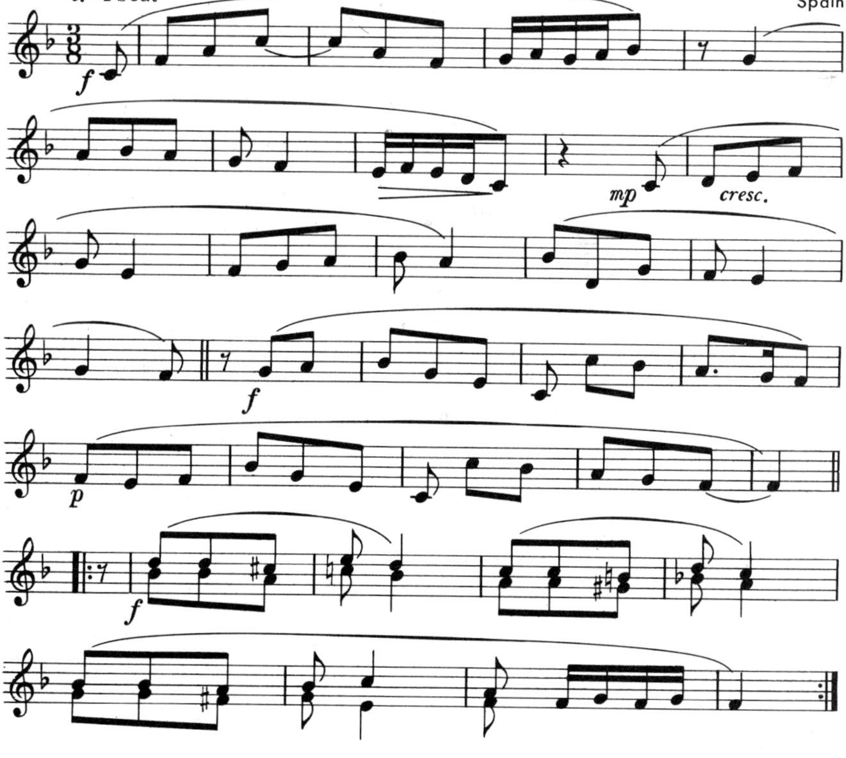

f

mp *cresc.*

f

p

f

Dvořák, Quartet, Op. 51

813

Haydn, Quartet, Op. 74, No. 1

814

Haydn, Quartet, Op. 20, No. 6

815

816

Handel, Trio Sonata, Op. 5, No. 4

817

(Allegro)

Handel, Sonata for Flute and Continuo

*

* Continuo may be sung and/or realized at the keyboard.

CHAPTER 15

MELODY

the medieval modes

The term *mode* refers to the arrangement of whole steps and half steps (or sometimes other intervals) to form a scale. In contrast to the present common use of major and minor modes, pre-seventeenth century music was largely based on a system of six different modes. These modes are also very common in folk music of the Western world. They were virtually neglected by composers of the seventeenth, eighteenth and nineteenth centuries, but have again found favor in the twentieth century by composers of both serious and popular music.

The modes used in this chapter are those known variously as the *church modes,* the *ecclesiastical modes,* or the *medieval modes.*

Mode	White-note scale on keyboard[1]	Characteristic
Aeolian	A	Same as natural (pure) minor
Ionian	C	Same as major
Dorian	D	Similar to natural minor but with a raised sixth scale step
Phrygian	E	Similar to natural minor with a lowered second scale step
Lydian	F	Similar to major with a raised fourth scale step
Mixolydian	G	Similar to major with a lowered seventh scale step

[1]A mode on B, sometimes called *Locrian,* was not useful because of the interval of a tritone between tonic and dominant.

As an example, the Dorian mode can be found by playing on the piano an ascending scale consisting of white keys only, starting on D. This results in a scale whose pattern of steps and half-steps differs from the patterns of the well-known major and minor scales. This Dorian scale sounds somewhat like a minor scale but differs from D minor in that the sixth scale step is B♮ rather than B♭. The Dorian mode on D, therefore, has a signature of no sharps and no flats, although it is often found with a signature of one flat (D minor) with B♮ indicated throughout the composition.

Modes can be transposed to begin on any pitch or letter name. To transpose the Dorian mode to G, as in melody 823, note that the minor mode on G has two flats; raising the sixth scale step cancels the E♭, leaving one flat (♭) in the scale.

A modal melody can be found with one or more scale steps not used, making positive identification of the mode impossible. A melody with the tonic note D, using the pitches D E F G A—C D, could be Dorian with B missing or transposed Aeolian with B♭ missing (see melody 827, scale F G A♭ B♭C—E♭ F).

A modal melody may include altered tones that are not part of the scale, for example, the neighboring note G♯ in measure 8 of melody 831.

Section 1. Single line melodies.

Aeolian mode: A B C D E F G A

Dorian mode: D E F G A B C D

Phrygian mode: E F G A B C D E

Lydian: F G A B C D E F

Mixolydian: G A B C D E F G

Dorian, transposed: G A B♭ C D E F G

mf
827
Andante
Scotland
f
mf
f
mf
mp
828
Allegro
England
mf
829
Jovially
England
f
1.
2.
p
cresc.
cresc.
f

830
Tempo giusto
Hungary (Bartók)
f

831
Allegretto
Andalusia
mp
mf
f
rit.
p

832
Brightly
Illinois
f
mf
rit.

Lento
Spain
833
p
rit.
Alla marcia
France
834
f
Canon for 3 voices
England
835
1.
2.
3.
Heigh - ho! An - y bod - y home? Food nor drink nor
mon-ey have we none, Yet we shall be mer - - ry.
Adagio
Scotland
836
mf
Fine
f
D.C. al Fine

Moderato
Spain
837
mp
mf
Con moto
Newfoundland
838
mp
mf
p
mf
Allegro moderato
England
839
mf
f
mf
Anon. (13th century)
840
p
Fine
mf
D.C.

Andante
England
841
Andante
Pennsylvania
842
Moderato
Rhode Island
843
cresc.
Moderato
Alec Rowley, O Lovely Babe
844

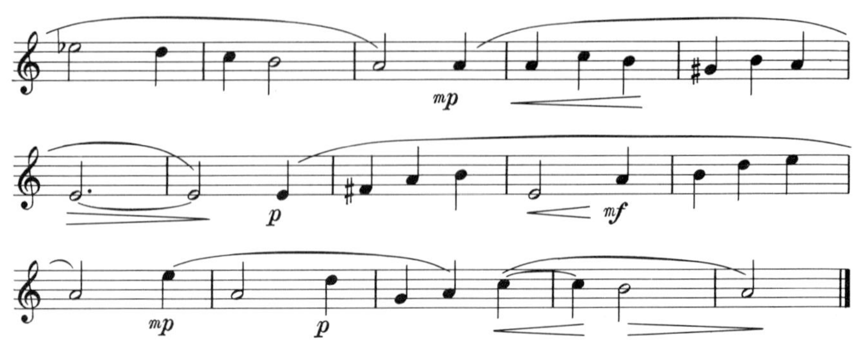
mp
p
mf
mp
p

Ravel, Chanson de la mariée
Moderato
845
p

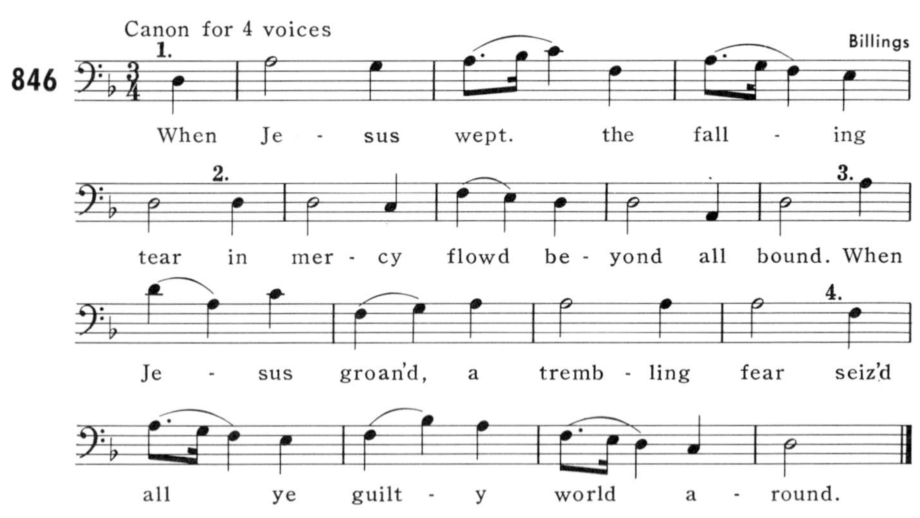
Canon for 4 voices
Billings
846
1.
When Je - sus wept. the fall - ing
2.
3.
tear in mer - cy flowd be - yond all bound. When
4.
Je - sus groan'd, a tremb - ling fear seiz'd
all ye guilt - y world a - round.

Section 2. Duets.

Lassus, *Crucifixus**

847
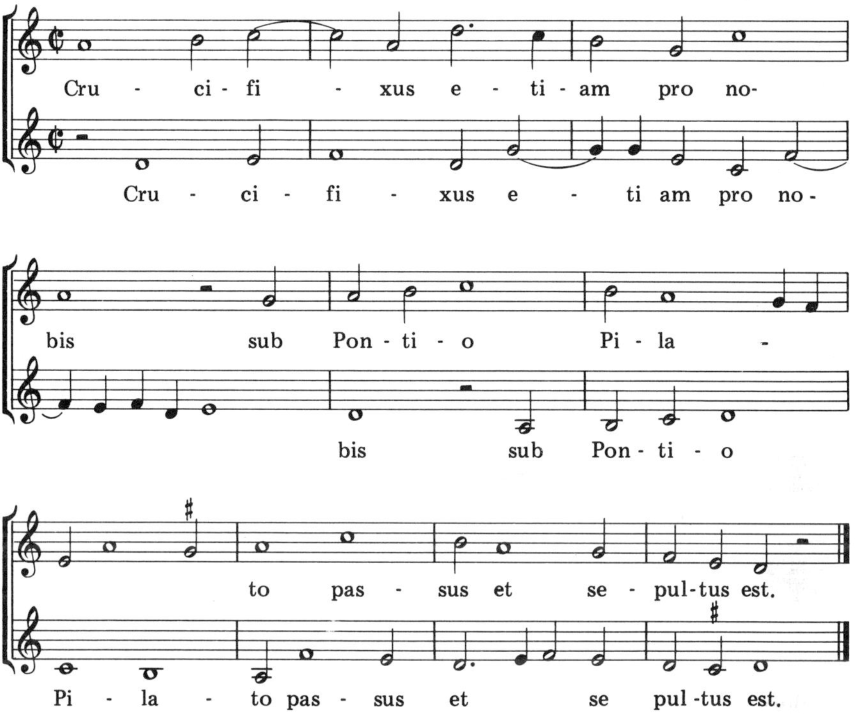
Cru - ci - fi - xus e - ti - am pro no-
Cru - ci - fi - xus e - ti am pro no -
bis sub Pon - ti - o Pi - la -
bis sub Pon - ti - o
to pas - sus et se - pul-tus est.
Pi - la - to pas - sus et se pul -tus est.

* For discussion of meter and *musica ficta* as used in this and following examples, see *Elementary Harmony, Theory and Practice,* pp. 139-142.

Josquin, *Missa ad Fugam*

848
Be - ne - di - ctus, be - ne - di - ctus.
Be - ne - di - ctus.
Be - ne - di -
Be - ne - di - ctus. Be - ne - di -

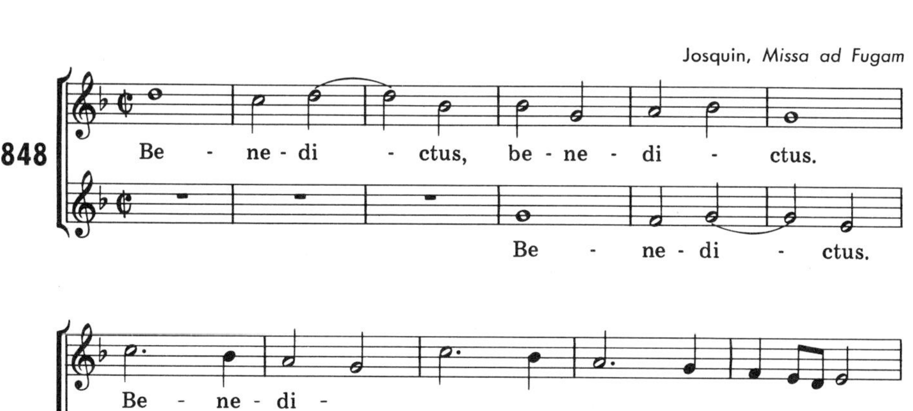

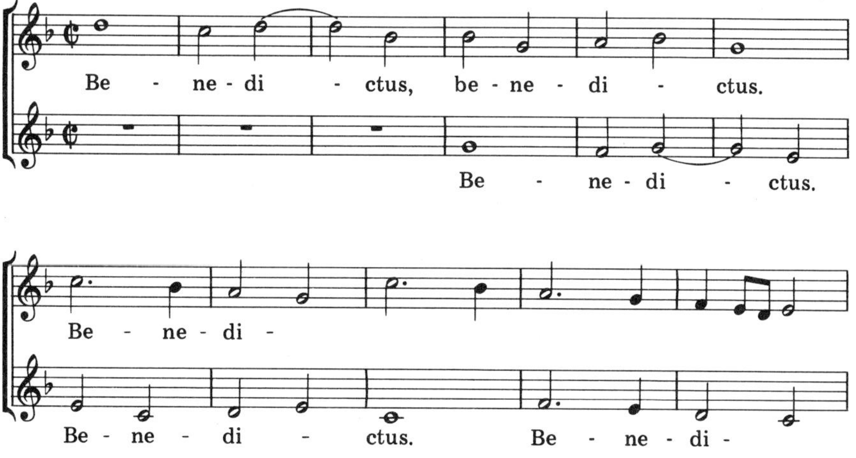

Victoria, *Magnificat Septimi Toni*

849

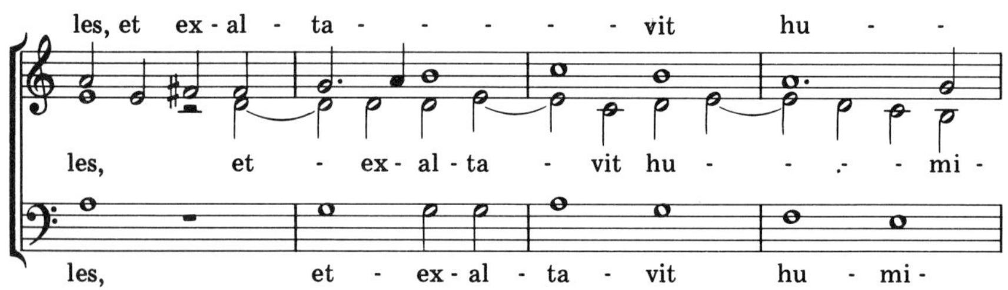

Palestrina, *Missa de Beata Virgine*

850

ri - a tu
a, glo - ri - a
a, glo - ri - a
a, glo - ri - a tu - a.
tu - a, glo - ri - a tu - a.
tu - a, glo - ri - a tu - a.

CHAPTER 16

RHYTHM

triplet division of undotted note values; duplet division of dotted note values

A triplet division of an undotted note value is indicated by three notes with a "3" added; these three use the same note value as the usual division into two parts (♩ = ♫ = [3 eighth notes, triplet 3]).

The duple division of a dotted note can be indicated in three ways:

1. Most commonly, two notes with a "2," using the next smaller note value (♩. = [3 eighth notes] = [2 eighth notes, duplet 2]).
2. Less commonly, two notes with a "2," using the same note value as the one being divided (♩. = [2 quarter notes, duplet 2]) See melody 914.
3. Found mostly in twentieth century music, two dotted notes of the next smaller value (𝅗𝅥. = ♩. ♩. and ♩. = [2 dotted eighth notes]), both of which can be seen in melody 1082, among others, in Chapter 21.

Triplet Division

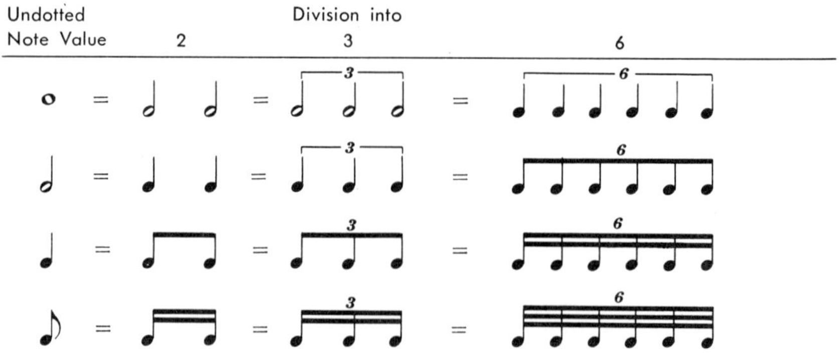

Undotted Note Value		Division into 2		3		6
𝅝	=	𝅗𝅥 𝅗𝅥	=	𝅗𝅥 𝅗𝅥 𝅗𝅥 (3)	=	♩ ♩ ♩ ♩ ♩ ♩ (6)
𝅗𝅥	=	♩ ♩	=	♩ ♩ ♩ (3)	=	♪ ♪ ♪ ♪ ♪ ♪ (6)
♩	=	♪ ♪	=	♪ ♪ ♪ (3)	=	𝅘𝅥𝅯 𝅘𝅥𝅯 𝅘𝅥𝅯 𝅘𝅥𝅯 𝅘𝅥𝅯 𝅘𝅥𝅯 (6)
♪	=	𝅘𝅥𝅯 𝅘𝅥𝅯	=	𝅘𝅥𝅯 𝅘𝅥𝅯 𝅘𝅥𝅯 (3)	=	𝅘𝅥𝅰 𝅘𝅥𝅰 𝅘𝅥𝅰 𝅘𝅥𝅰 𝅘𝅥𝅰 𝅘𝅥𝅰 (6)

Duplet Division

Dotted Note Value		3		Division into 2		4
𝅝.	=	𝅗𝅥 𝅗𝅥 𝅗𝅥	=	²𝅗𝅥 𝅗𝅥	=	⁴♩ ♩ ♩ ♩
𝅗𝅥.	=	♩ ♩ ♩	=	²♩ ♩	=	⁴♪ ♪ ♪ ♪
♩.	=	♪ ♪ ♪	=	²♪ ♪	=	⁴𝅘𝅥𝅯 𝅘𝅥𝅯 𝅘𝅥𝅯 𝅘𝅥𝅯
♪.	=	𝅘𝅥𝅯 𝅘𝅥𝅯 𝅘𝅥𝅯	=	²𝅘𝅥𝅯 𝅘𝅥𝅯	=	⁴𝅘𝅥𝅰 𝅘𝅥𝅰 𝅘𝅥𝅰 𝅘𝅥𝅰

RHYTHMIC READING

Section 1. Triplet division of undotted note values.

Examples (*a*) and (*b*) are identical in sound when the duration of each of the beat-note values is the same.

856

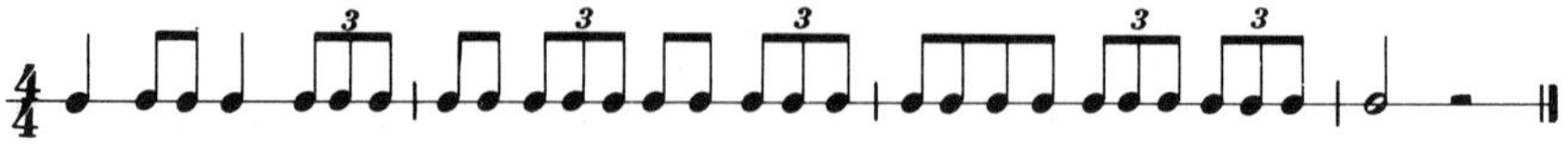

857

858

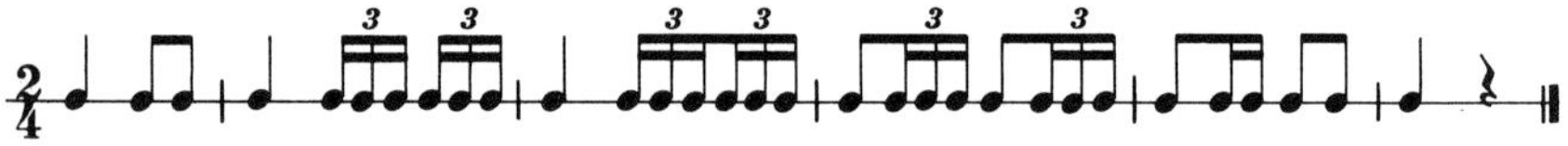

859

860

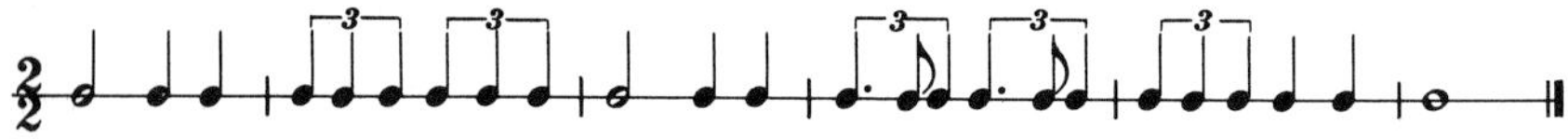

861

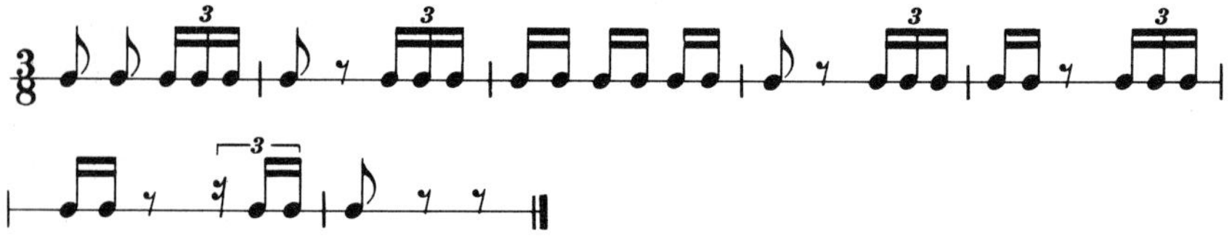

862

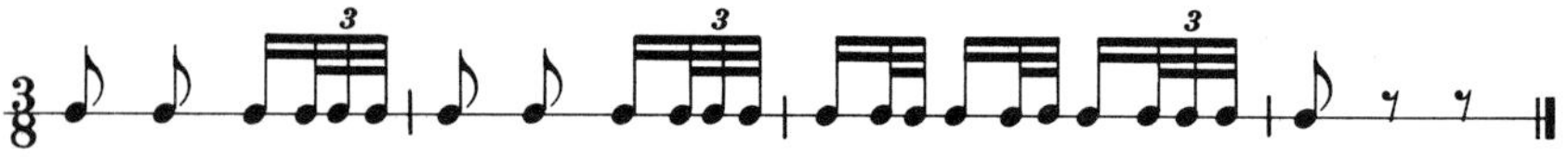

Section 2. Duplet division of dotted note values.

Examples (*a*) and (*b*) are identical in sound when the duration of each of the beat-note values is the same.

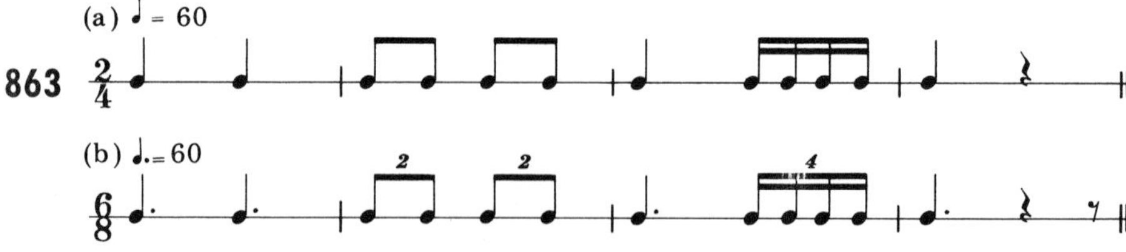

Section 3. Two-part drills.

873

874
875
876
877
878
879
880
881

SIGHT SINGING

Section 4. Triplet division of undotted note values.

885 Con spirito — Arizona

f *ff* *f* *mf* *mp* *cresc.* *f* *ff*

Mendelssohn, *O for the Wings of a Dove*

886 Con moto

Schumann, *Frühlingsbotschaft*, Op. 79, No. 3

887 Schnell

Andante
Wagner, Rienzi
888
Schubert, Wasserflut, Op. 89, No. 6
Langsam
889
(stark)
Schubert, Am Strome, Op. 8 No. 4
Moderato
890

Handel, *Samson*

Allegro

891

p f mf p f

Chopin, *Mazurka*, Op. 7, No. 4

Presto ma non troppo

892

Sostenuto
Giordano, Fedora
893
Slowly
California
894
Allegro
Spain
895
cresc.

cresc.
Franz, Liebchen ist da
Andantino
896

Portug
Andante
897
rit.

Portug
Langsam
898

899 With breadth and vigor — Byrd, *Make Ye Joy to the World*

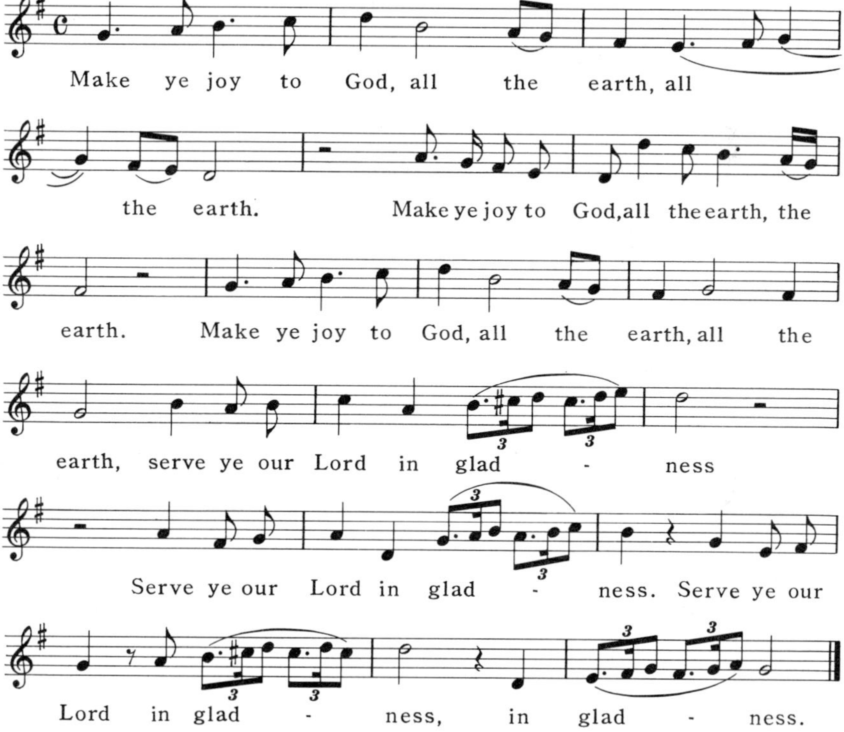

Make ye joy to God, all the earth, all the earth. Make ye joy to God, all the earth, the earth. Make ye joy to God, all the earth, all the earth, serve ye our Lord in glad - ness

Serve ye our Lord in glad - ness. Serve ye our Lord in glad - ness, in glad - ness.

900 Con spirito — Mexico

f *Fine*

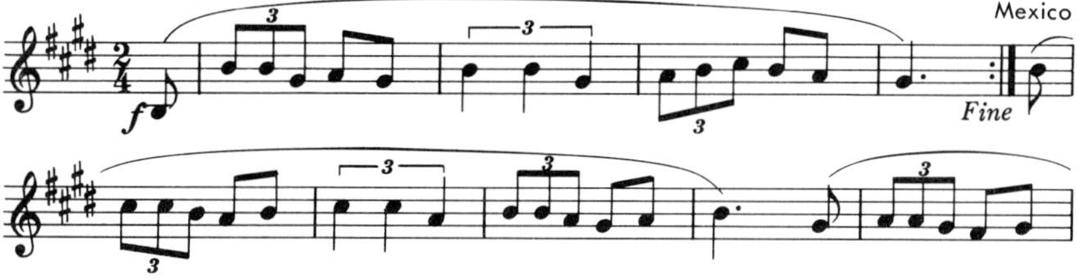

D.C.
Moderato
Costa Rica
901
Allegro
Spain
902
Allegro assai
Berlioz, Les Troyens à Carthage
903
Slowly
Spiritual, United States
904

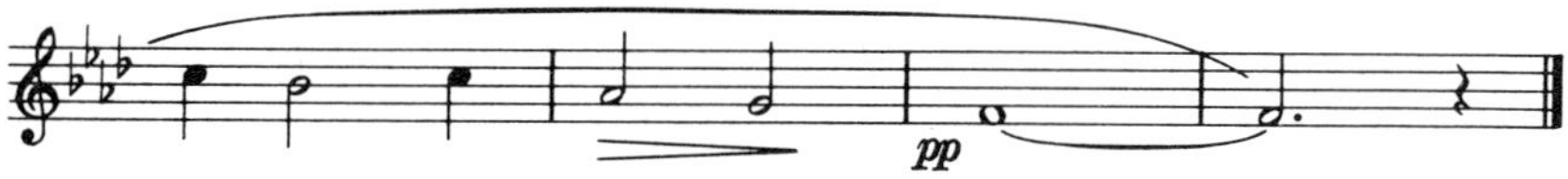

Adagio — Slovakia

905

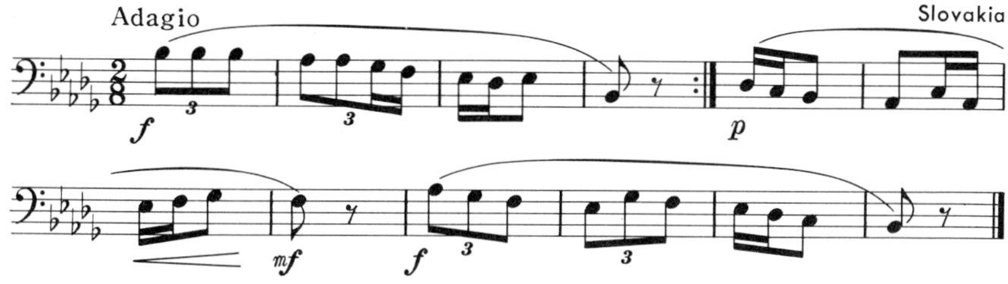

Andante con moto — Venezuela

906

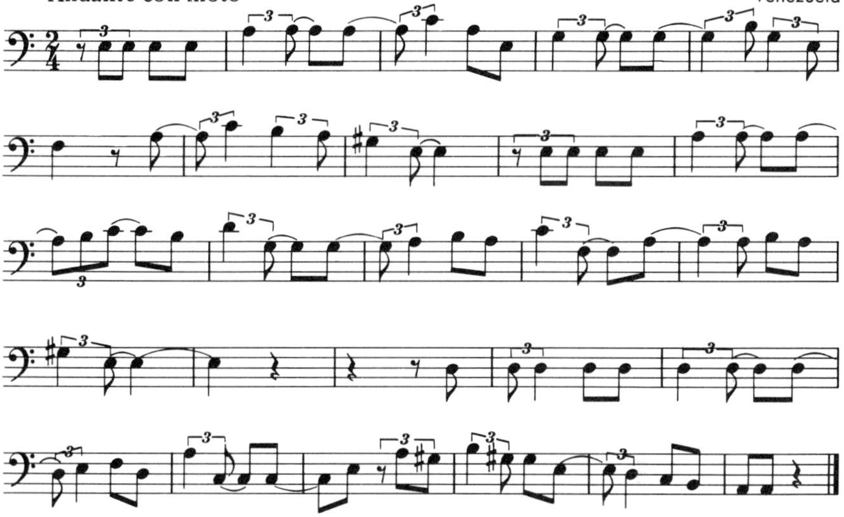

Section 5. Duplet division of dotted note values. Other divisions.

Moderato — Utah

907

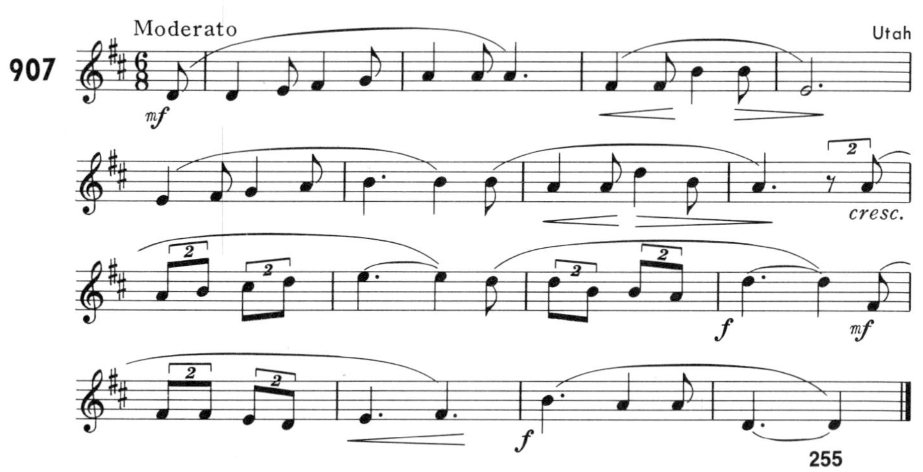

Allegro
Grieg, Das Dichters Gesang
908
mf
Assez animé
France
909
f
Moderato
Pennsylvania
910
mp
♪. = 108
Texas
911
f

Moderato
Mexico
912
Lebhaft
Brahms, *Guter Rat*, Op. 75
913
Brückler (1845–1871), *Als ich zum erstenmal dich sah*
Herzlich
914
Franz, *Genesung*
Allegro
915

f
poco rit.

916

Allegro appassionato
Grieg, To Spring
pp
fz
rit.
p
a tempo
rit.
f

917

Lento
Spain
mf
mp

Schumann, Der schwere Abend,
Op. 90, No. 6
♩ = 104
918
Modéré et gracieux
France
919
Allegro
Spain
920

Section 6. Duets.

Con moto
Germany
926
Andantino
Germany
927

Cornelius, Lied des Narren
928
Langsam
a tempo
poco rit.
a tempo
Brahms, String Quartet, Op. 88
929
Grave
cresc.
Binchois (c.1400-1460), Missa Angelorum
930
Andante
Et in spir - i - tum sanc - tum Do - mi -
Et in spir - i - tum sanc - tum Do - mi -

num et vi - vi - fi - -
num et vi -
can - tem qui ex - pa - tre
vi - fi - can - tem qui ex pa -
fi - li - o - que pro - ce - dit.
tre fi - li - o - que pro - ce - dit.
Allegretto
Schumann, *Faust*, Op. 148
931
sempre p
sempre p

3
mf
mf

CHAPTER 17

RHYTHM

changing time signatures; less common time signatures; the hemiola

RHYTHMIC READING

Section 1. Definitions[1] and reading exercises.

(a) Variable Meters. The time signature is changed as needed throughout the composition. See melody 948.

[1]Some of this terminology is from Gardner Read, *Music Notation* (Boston: Allyn & Bacon, 1969).

(b) Alternating Meters with Double or Triple Time Signatures. A double time signature, such as $\frac{2}{4}\,\frac{3}{4}$, usually indicates regular alternation of the two signatures ($\frac{2}{4}\,\frac{3}{4}\,\frac{2}{4}\,\frac{3}{4}$ etc.) or some other regular pattern ($\frac{2}{4}\,\frac{3}{4}\,\frac{3}{4}\,\frac{2}{4}\,\frac{3}{4}\,\frac{3}{4}$ etc.). See melodies 947 and 957; for triple time signature, see melody 955.

(c) Combined Meters. When the change of time signature is from simple to compound time, or reverse, a directive usually occurs at the location of the first change. At measure two in exercise 938 below, the directive ♩ = ♩. means that the ♩. note of the $\frac{6}{8}$ measure is equal in duration to the ♩ note of the preceding measure.[2] See melodies 952 and 954.

When the number of beat divisions in each meter is the same, the durations of the divisions are usually equal, and no directive is required (exercise 939). The measures of exercise 940 below are of equal duration; measures 1 and 2 are differentiated by the location of the accent. See melody 959.

[2]In many older editions of music, the directive is often reversed: ♩ = ♩. means that the ♩ of the following measure equals the ♩. of the preceding measure.

(d) Meters of 5 and 7 (Quintuple Simple and Septuple Simple Meters). These time signatures usually simply replace an alternating meter: $\frac{5}{4} = \frac{3}{4}\,\frac{2}{4}$ or $\frac{2}{4}\,\frac{3}{4}$; $\frac{7}{8} = \frac{4}{8}\,\frac{3}{8}$ or $\frac{3}{8}\,\frac{4}{8}$. For an example of quintuple compound meter, see melody 961, written in the alternating meters of $\frac{9}{8}$ and $\frac{6}{8}$. By combining each pair of nine- and six-beat measures, a signature of $\frac{15}{8}$ could have been used.

Numerators other than 5, 7, and the common ones already studied are quite rare in music before the twentieth century; they must be interpreted on an individual basis.

(e) The Hemiola. A pattern wherein two successive groups of three beats or beat divisions are so accented that they become three groups of two, or, less commonly, the reverse.

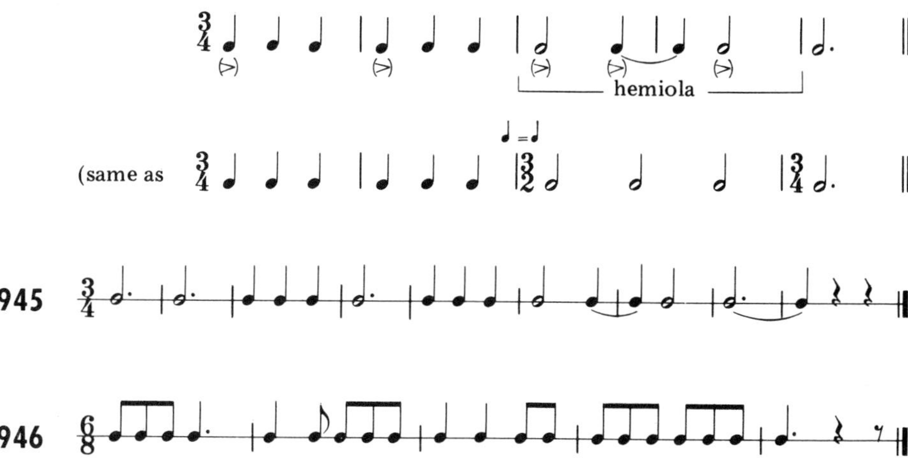

Section 2. Changing time signatures.

951
Allegro
France
mp
f
952
Allegro
Jamaica
f
mf
953
Tempo giusto
Hungary (Bartók)
f
954
Langsamer
Schumann, *Jemand*, Op. 25, No. 4
p
f
p
f

955
Pas vite
France
f
956
Allegro
Czechoslovakia
f
mf
f
957
Con moto
Brahms, Agnes, Op. 59, No. 5
poco f
p
poco f
p
poco f
p
poco f
958
Canon for 3 voices
Byrd
1.
2.
3.
Hey ho! to the Green - wood now let us
go. Sing heave and ho. And there will we
*

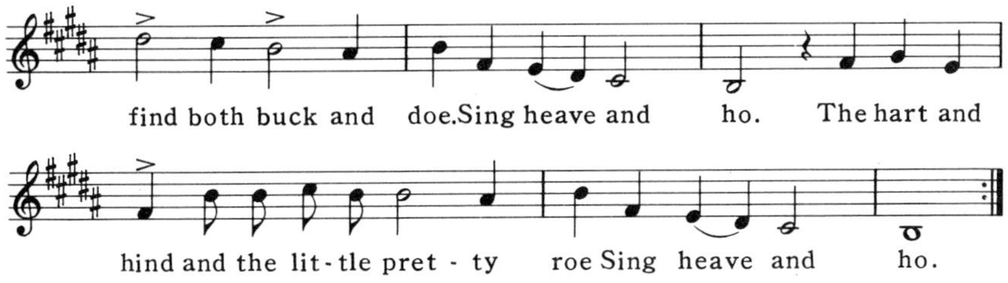

* Canon may end at this point.

959 Molto lento e sostenuto

De Falla, *El Retablo de Maese Pedro*

$\frac{3}{4} = \frac{6}{8}$

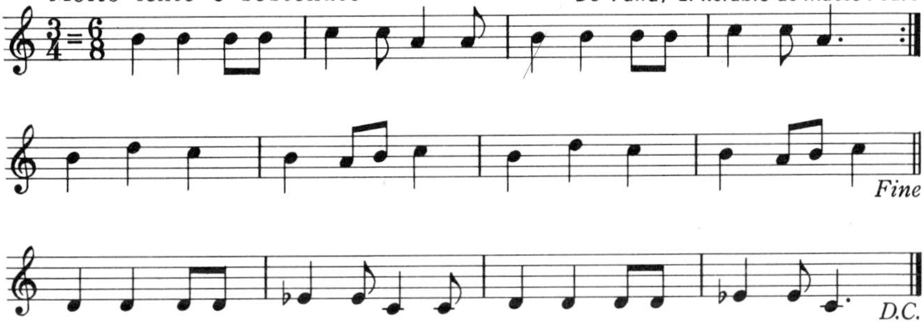

Fine

D.C.

960 Canon for 3 voices

J. Nares (18th century)

1

Wilt thou lend me thy mare to go a mile?

No! she's lame leap-ing o - ver a style.

2

But if thou wilt her to me spare,

Thou shalt have mon - ey for thy mare.

3

Oh! ho! say you so?

Mon-ey will make my mare to go; Mon-ey will make my mare to go!

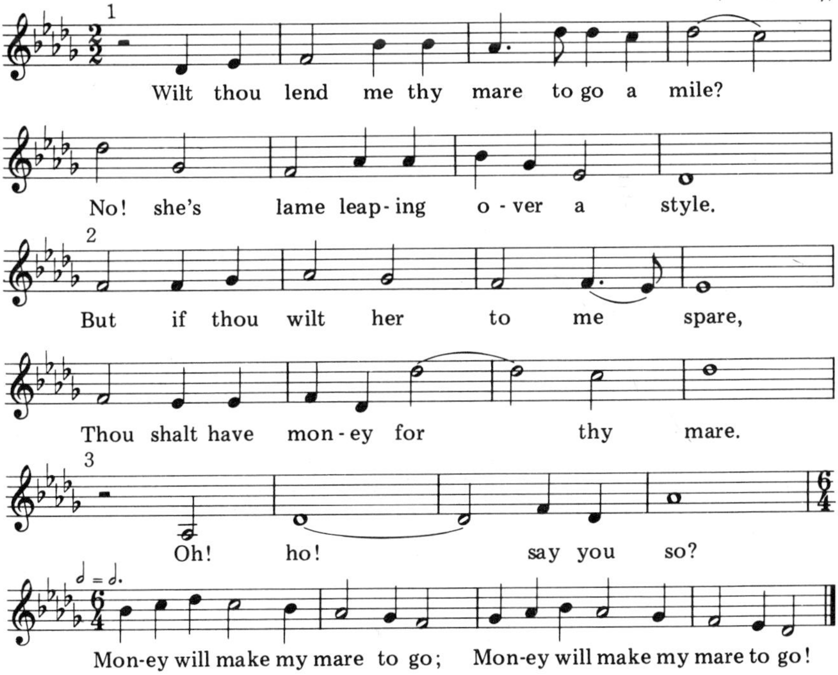

961

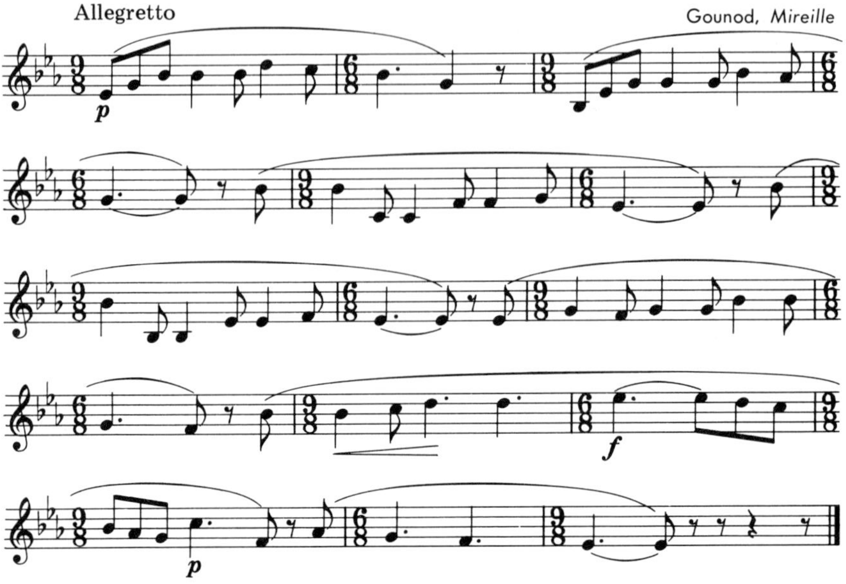

Allegretto
Gounod, *Mireille*
p
f
p

962

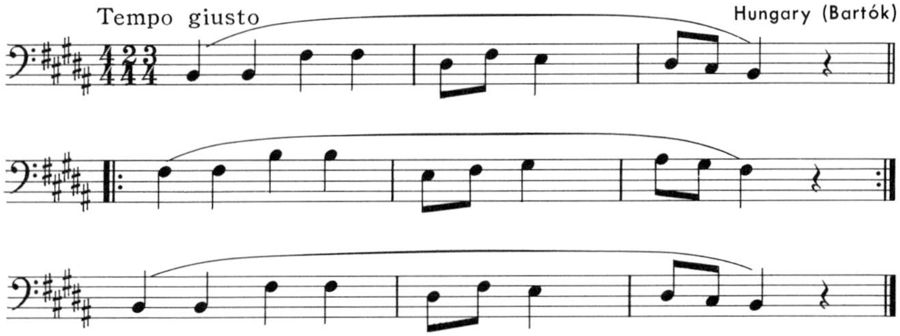

Tempo giusto
Hungary (Bartók)

The next two examples from the late sixteenth century were written without bar lines. The added bar lines have been placed to coincide with the principal accents of the text.

963

Largo
Tallis (1567), Why Fumeth in Sight?*
p
(Melody in Tenor)
Why fumeth in sight the Gen - tiles
p

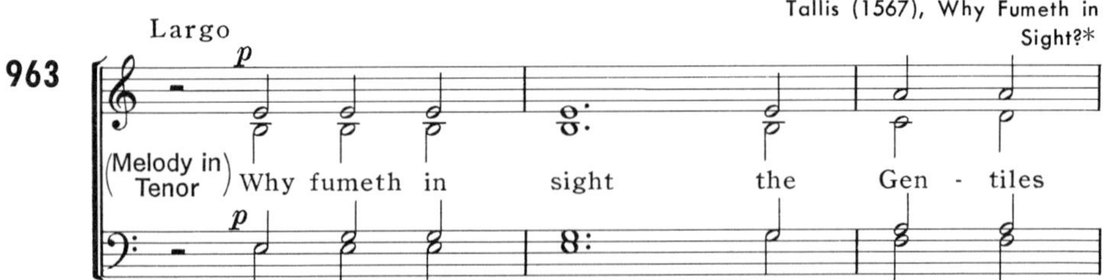

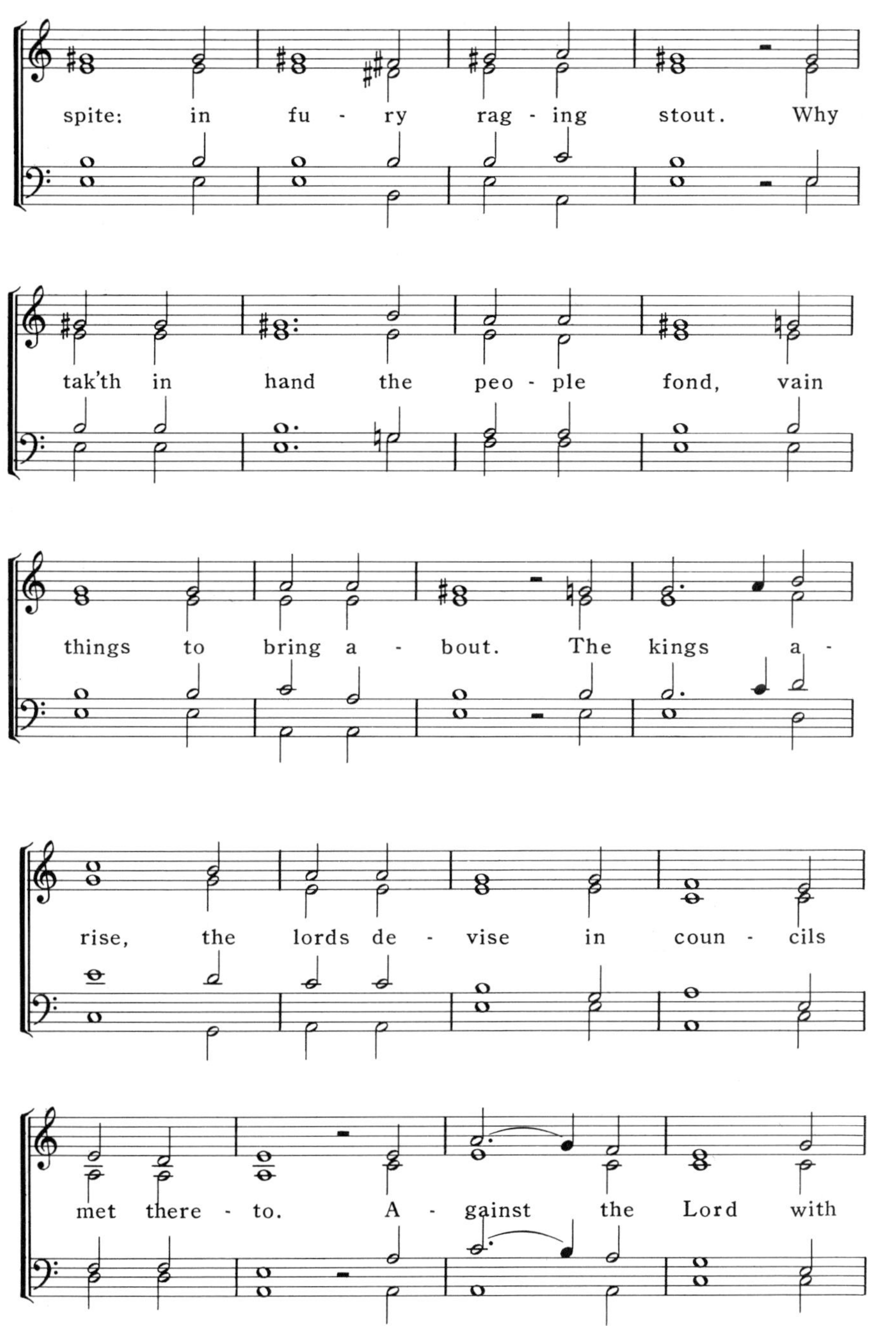

*This melody is used by Ralph Vaughan Williams in his "Fantasia on a Theme of Thomas Tallis."

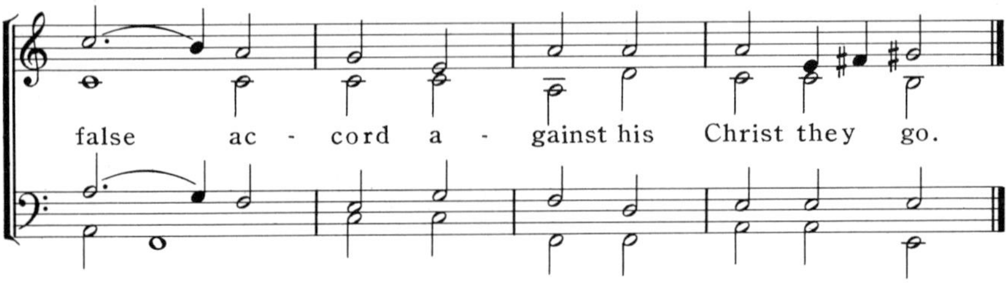
false ac - cord a - gainst his Christ they go.

Dowland (1597), Can She Excuse My Wrongs?

Rather slow

964

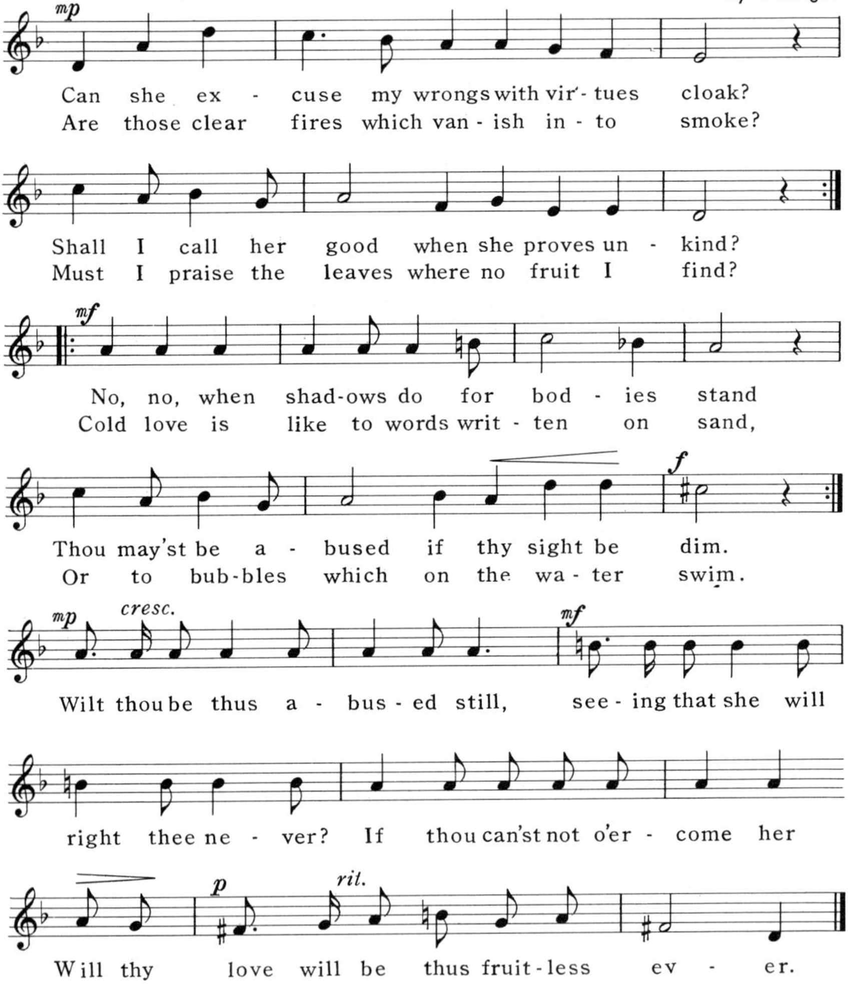
mp
Can she ex - cuse my wrongs with vir - tues cloak?
Are those clear fires which van - ish in - to smoke?
Shall I call her good when she proves un - kind?
Must I praise the leaves where no fruit I find?
mf
No, no, when shad-ows do for bod - ies stand
Cold love is like to words writ - ten on sand,
f
Thou may'st be a - bused if thy sight be dim.
Or to bub-bles which on the wa - ter swim.
mp
cresc.
mf
Wilt thou be thus a - bus - ed still, see - ing that she will
right thee ne - ver? If thou can'st not o'er - come her
p
rit.
Will thy love will be thus fruit-less ev - er.

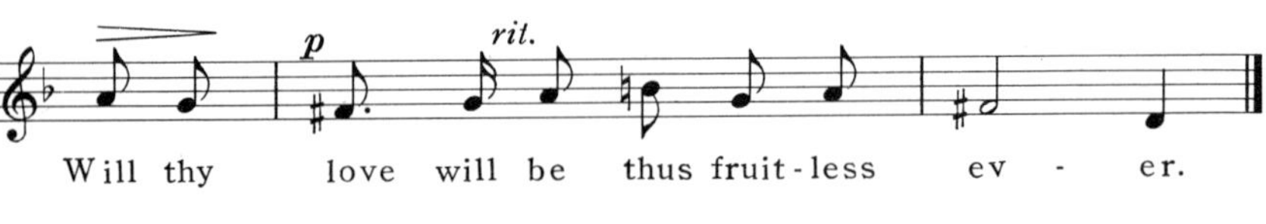

Section 3. Meters of 5 and 7, and other meters.

969
Moderato
Mexico
mf
970
Canon for 3 voices
Germany
1.
2.
3.
971
Allegro spiritoso
Greece
f
1.
2.
972
Allegro moderato
Croatia
f
1.
2.

Vivo
Venezuela
973
mf
f
p
mf
p
Moderato
Mexico
974
mf
Molto moderato
Elgar, Caractacus
975
p
3
O my war- ri - ors tell me tru - ly
o'er the red graves where ye lie. That your
mon-arch led you du- ly, first to charge and last to fly.
O my war - ri - ors!

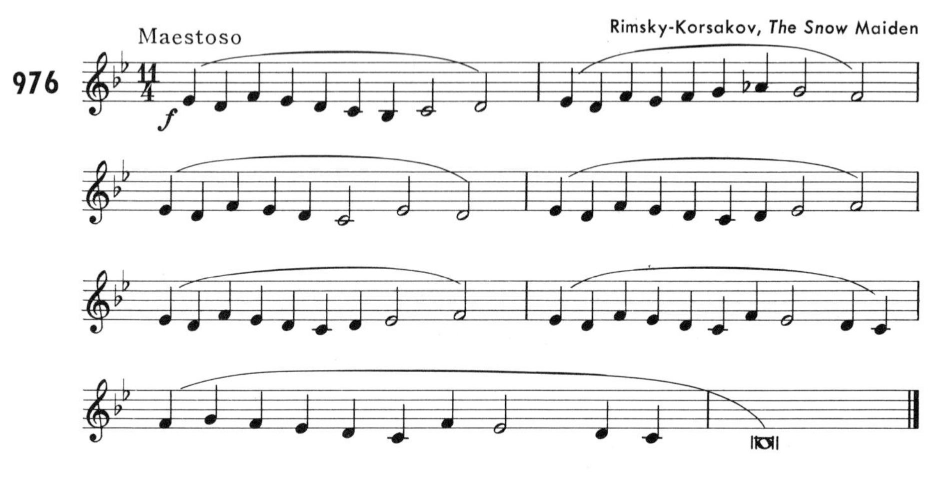
976
Maestoso
Rimsky-Korsakov, The Snow Maiden
f

977
Andantino (♩ = 84)
Moussorgsky, Boris Godunov
mf

978
Adagio
Spain
mp
mf

Section 4. The hemiola.

982
Bach, Motet, Jesu meine Freude
C minor: V7/iv
983
Allegro
Bach, Brandenburg Concerto, No. 4
f
p
cresc.
f
p
cresc.
f
984
Adagio
Haydn, Piano Sonata (1776)
985
Im Ländler tempo
Brahms, Liebeslieder Walzer, Op. 52, No. 2
f
p

Allegro molto
Spain
986
Allegro non troppo
Brahms, Symphony No. 2, Op. 73
987

CHAPTER 18

RHYTHM

further subdivision of the beat; notation in slow tempi

The use of note values smaller than the divisions presented in previous chapters is relatively uncommon. The two such uses are:

1. The beat note is divided into eight parts in simple time (more than eight parts are possible but rare):

2. The division of the beat (as indicated by the time signature) is used as the beat-note value. When the tempo of a composition is very slow, the time signature often does not actually express the number of beats in the measure. In a very slow $\frac{2}{4}$ measure, for example, there will actually be four beats, the eighth note receiving one beat. Similarly, in a very slow tempo, the numerator of the time signature for a compound meter actually indicates the number of beats in the measure. Consequently, in a slow $\frac{6}{8}$, instead of two ♩. beats in one measure, there will be six ♪ beats in one measure.

When to use the beat division as the actual beat note is sometimes difficult to ascertain. Beginning with Beethoven, who first made use of the metronome, composers at times include a metronome marking for the beat division, as in melody 1009, where the eighth note receives the beat in $\frac{2}{4}$ time, and in melody 1010, where, with the same time signature, the sixteenth note is designated as the beat.

When no marking is supplied by the composer, an editorial marking in parentheses is sometimes included in the score, as in melody 1013. Such a marking is based on the composer's tempo indication, or through knowledge of the composer's style and of historical performance precedents. When not indicated, the beat-note value must be similarly determined by the performer. But there will always be borderline cases where a slight difference in opinion can result in a difference in the choice of a beat-note value.

Section 1. Rhythmic reading.

(a) Read each example, using these metronome markings:

988-993 M.M. ♩ = 50
994-995 M. M. 𝅗𝅥 = 50
996-997 M. M. ♪ = 46

(b) Read each example, again using these metronome markings:

988-993 M. M. ♪ = 76
994-995 M. M. ♩ = 76
996-997 M. M. 𝅘𝅥𝅯 = 86

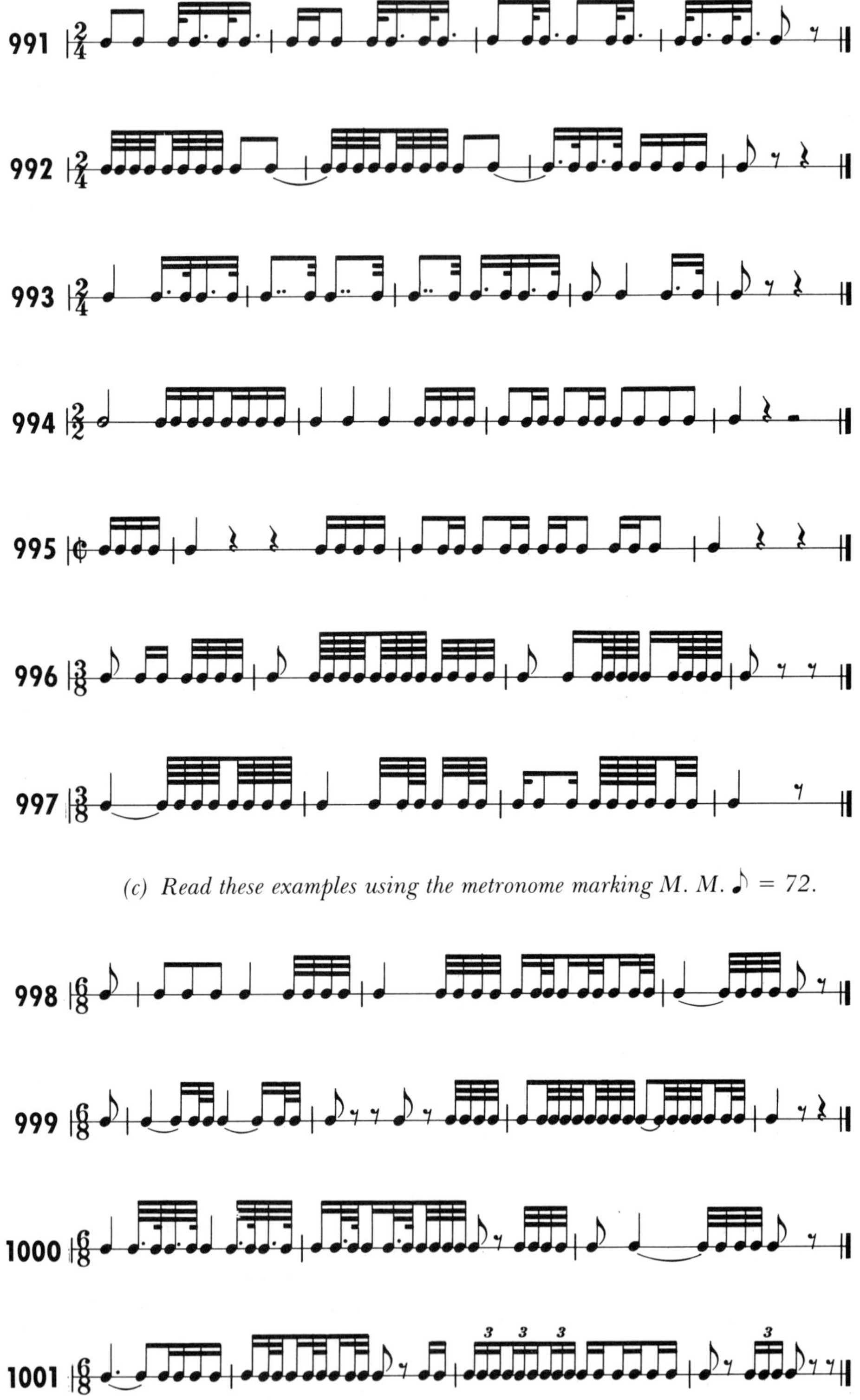

(c) Read these examples using the metronome marking M. M. ♪ *= 72.*

Section 2. Sight singing.

1006

1007

1008

fz *p*

fz

Beethoven, Quartet No. 2, Op. 18, No.2

Adagio cantabile ♪ = 72

1009

p

cresc.

Beethoven, Quartet No. 7, Op. 59, No.1

Adagio molto e mesto ♪ = 88

1010

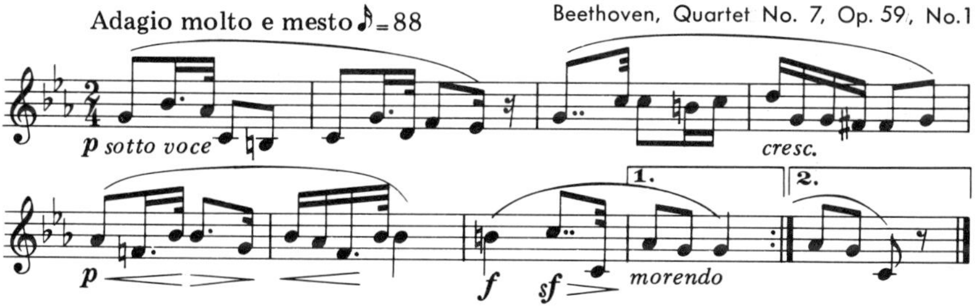

p sotto voce *cresc.*

p *f* *sf* *morendo*

1. 2.

Verdi, *La Traviata*

Allegro

1011

Spohr, Double Quartet, Op. 87

Andante

1012

Andante cantabile (♪= 80)
Donizetti, Don Pasquale
1013
mf
pp
cresc.
p
cresc.
p
p
mf
p
mf
mp
mf
p
rit.
mf a tempo

Händel, Athalia
Largo (♪= 72)
1014
p dolce
cresc.
mp
mp
rit.
Marcello, Lontananza e gelosia
Adagio (♪= 72)
1015
p

poco rit.
Andante con moto
Schubert, Symphony No. 5
p
Andante
Haydn, The Creation
p

1016

1017

Adagio
Haydn, Symphony No. 57
1018
p
Sostenuto (♪= 72)
Piccini, La buona figliuola
1019
mp
mf
f
mp
cresc.

rit.

CHAPTER 19

MELODY

Chromaticism (III); additional uses of chromatic intervals; remote modulation

Section 1. Chromatic intervals.

Diminished and augmented intervals, other than the augmented fourth and diminished fifth used in the V^7 chord, occasionally appear in melodic writing. These include the augmented second, the diminished third, the diminished fourth, and the diminished seventh.

The presence of a lowered second scale degree (D♭ in C major or C minor) often indicates the use of the Neapolitan triad, a major triad with the lowered second scale degree as its root (in C major or C minor, D♭ F A♭), symbolized by "N" or "♭ II)."

fp
p
Canon for 3 voices
Caldara
1022
1.
2.
3.
Andante con moto
Bizet, La jolie fille de Perth
1023
pp
pp
poco cresc.
p
Lento
France
1024
mp
Fine
mf
D.C.

Moderato
Haydn, Theresien-Messe
1025
Mozart, Minuet, K. 355
1026
dolce
f
p
f
p
f
p
Canon for 3 voices
Couperin
1027
1.
2.
3.
Allegro (𝅗𝅥. = 1 beat)
Mozart, Cosi fan tutte, K. 588
1028

Allegretto
Italy
1029
* Interval of a diminished third.
Grazioso
Rimsky-Korsakov, The Snow Maiden
1030
Allegro ben moderato
Meyerbeer, L'Africaine
1031

Mässig

Schubert, *Der Müller und der Bach*

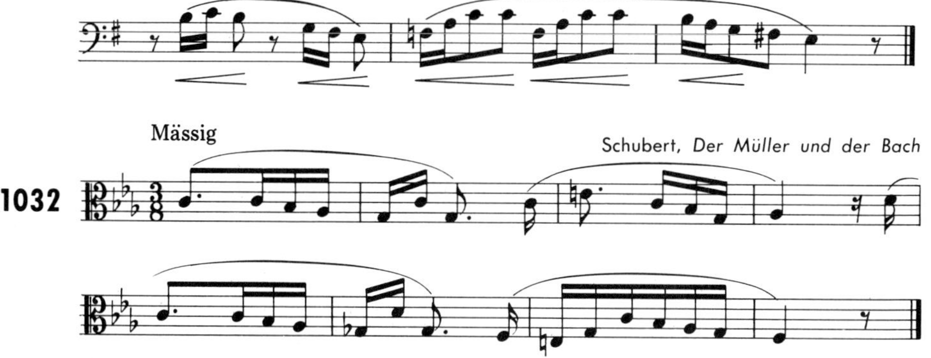

1032

Section 2. Remote modulation.

A modulation to any key other than a closely related key is known as a *remote* (or *foreign,* or *distant*) modulation.

Schubert, *Spät schon, wenn schon längst*

Langsam

1033 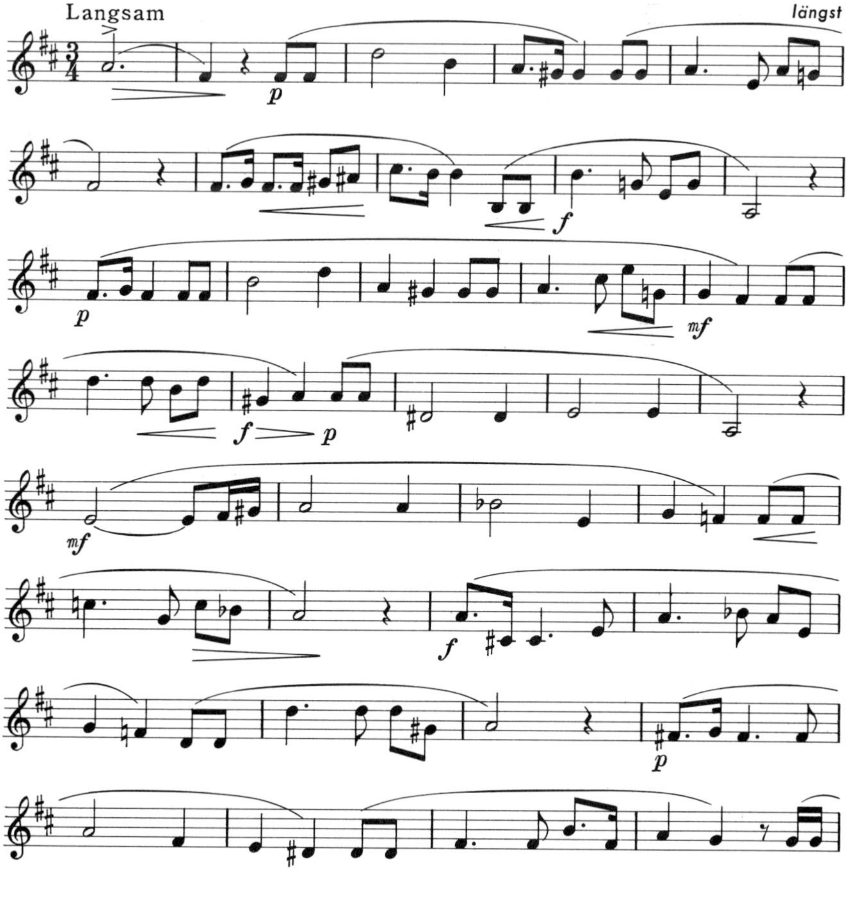

f
Langsam
Schubert, Wehmut Op. 22, No. 2
1034
p
p
p
mf
p
Schubert, Jüngling am Bache, Op. 87, No. 3
Mässig
1035
p
cresc.
mf
mp
mf
decresc.
rit.
p
Moderato
Mahler, Rhine Legend*
1036
p

rit. a tempo

poco rit. molto rit. a tempo

riten. a tempo

* Copyright 1914 by Universal Edition, Vienna. Copyright renewed 1941 by Alma Mahler-Werfel.

1037 Andante poco mosso — Offenbach, *Tales of Hoffman*

poco animato
f
allarg.
ff
Lento
a tempo
pp
rall.
Berlioz, The Damnation of Faust
Andante con moto
1038
p
sf

Berlioz, The Damnation of Faust
Allegro
1039
f
Allegretto grazioso
Brahms, Ständchen, Op. 106, No. 1
1040
p
Fine

cresc.
f
p
D.S.
Langsam
Schubert, Sehnsucht
1041
Andante
Mendelssohn, Keine von der Erde schönen, Op.post
1042
p
sf
p
sf
cresc.
p
dim.
cresc.
f
p
p
cresc.
f
sempre f
p

dolce
Waltz tempo
Schubert, Waltz, Op. 9, No. 14
1043
p
mf
Moderato poco animato
Saint-Saëns, Les Barbares
1044
Andante
Mussorgsky, Khovanschchina
1045

Langsam
Schumann, Dein Angesicht, Op. 127, No. 2
1046
p
rit.
p
rit.
In tempo
rit.
Adagio
Schubert, Mass in A♭ major
1047
pp
f
pp
f
pp
f
f

CHAPTER 20

SUPPLEMENTARY MATERIAL

longer melodic lines

1048 

mp
pp
cresc.
f
3
mp
cresc.
f
D.C.
Canon for 2 voices
Allegro moderato
Cherubini
1049
1
2

1050
Andante
Couperin, Brunette
p
mf
1.
2.
p

1.
2.
p
3
mf
p
mf
p
3
p
3
mf
3
p

p
1.
p
2.
p
pp
3
3
mp

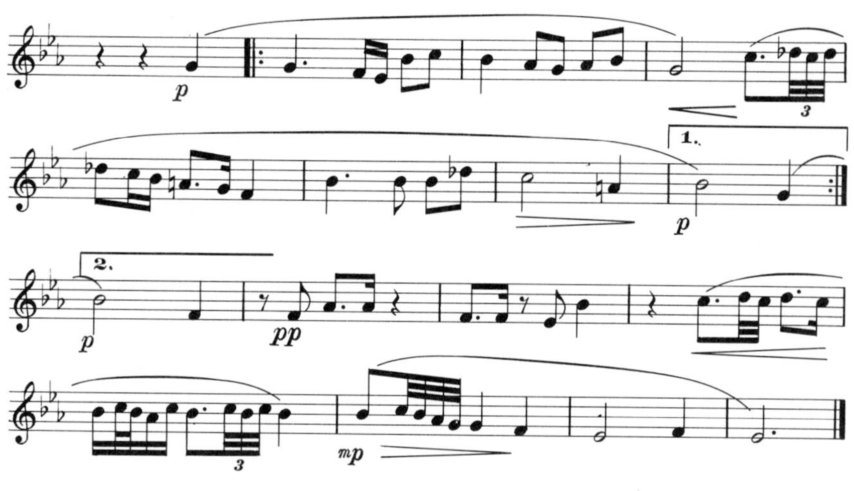

Allegretto

Bach, Cantata No. 206

1051

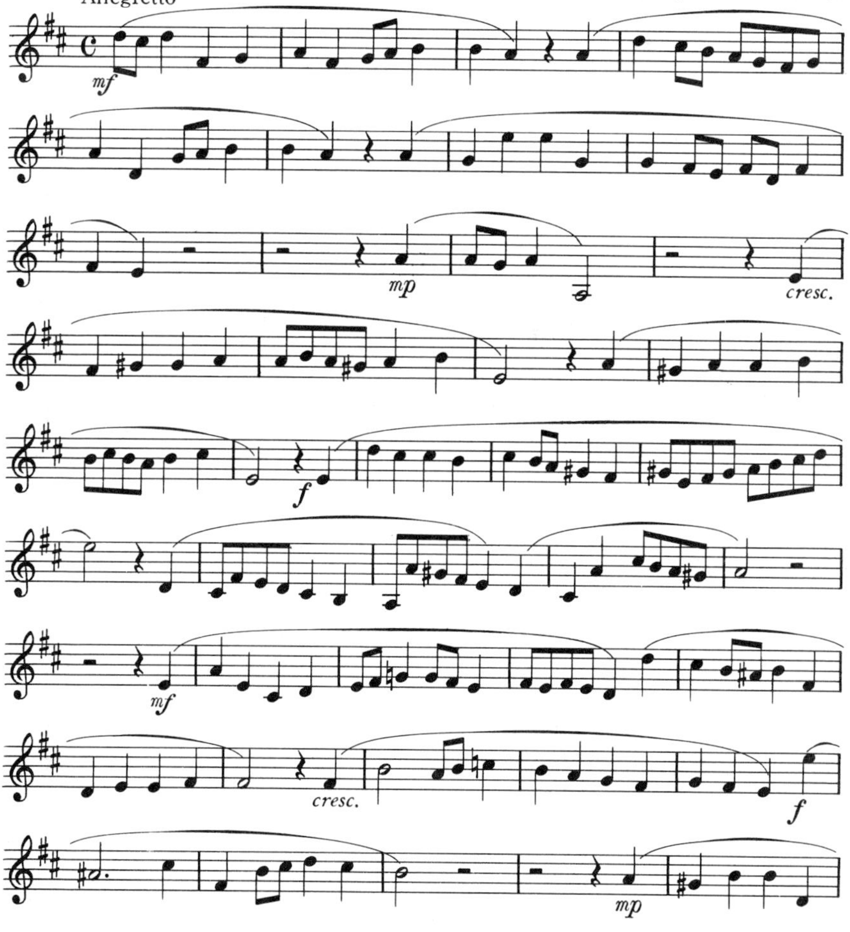
mf
mp
cresc.
f
mf
cresc.
f
mp

mf
rit.

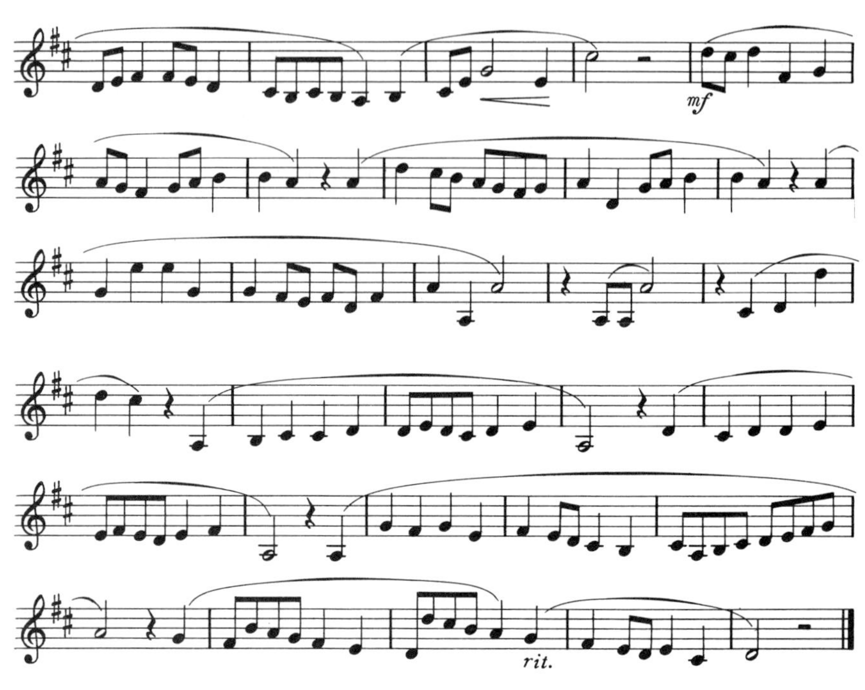

Bach, Cantata No. 35

Adagio (♪ = 76)

1052

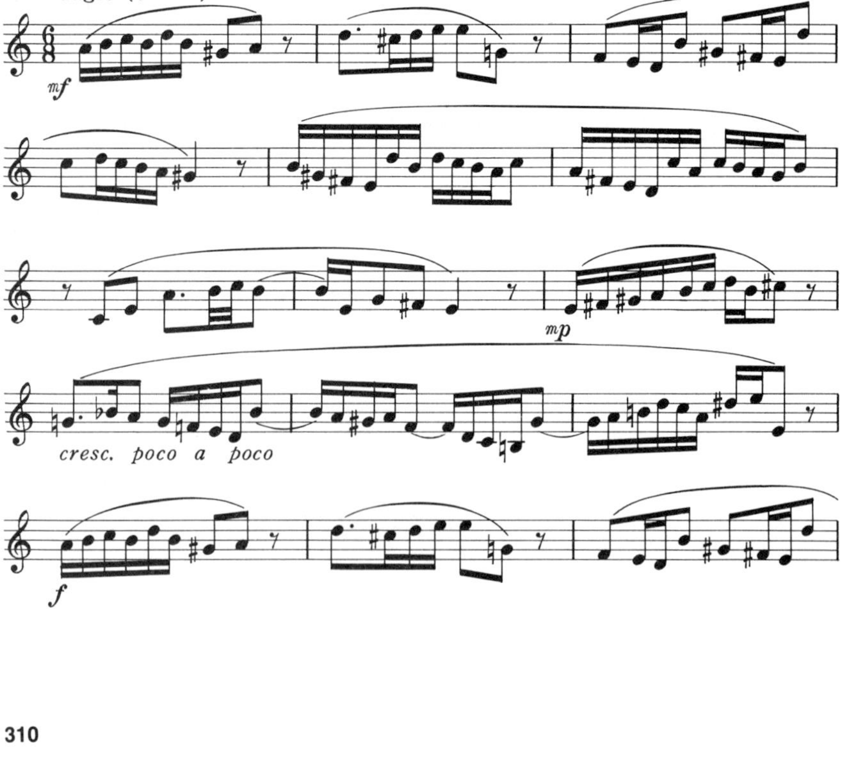
mf
mp
cresc. poco a poco
f

Fine

D.C. al Fine

Bach, Cantata No. 11

1053

2.
mp cresc.
mf
3
mp
mf

Handel, Solo Cantata No. 49

Largo

1054

mf

mp

mf

1055
Canon for 6 voices
Beethoven
1.
2.
3.
4.
5.
6.
1056
Andante maestoso
Rossini, The Barber of Seville

Lento
Liszt, Die drei Zigeuner
1057
mf
cresc.
Allegro vivace
p
Un poco più lento
mf
p
f molto accentuato

ff
Moderato
Hugo Wolf, Der Freund
1058
p dolce
poco rit.
a tempo
ff
p
ff
p
p
ff
Allegro moderato (♩ = 84)
Fauré, Mandoline
1059
dolce

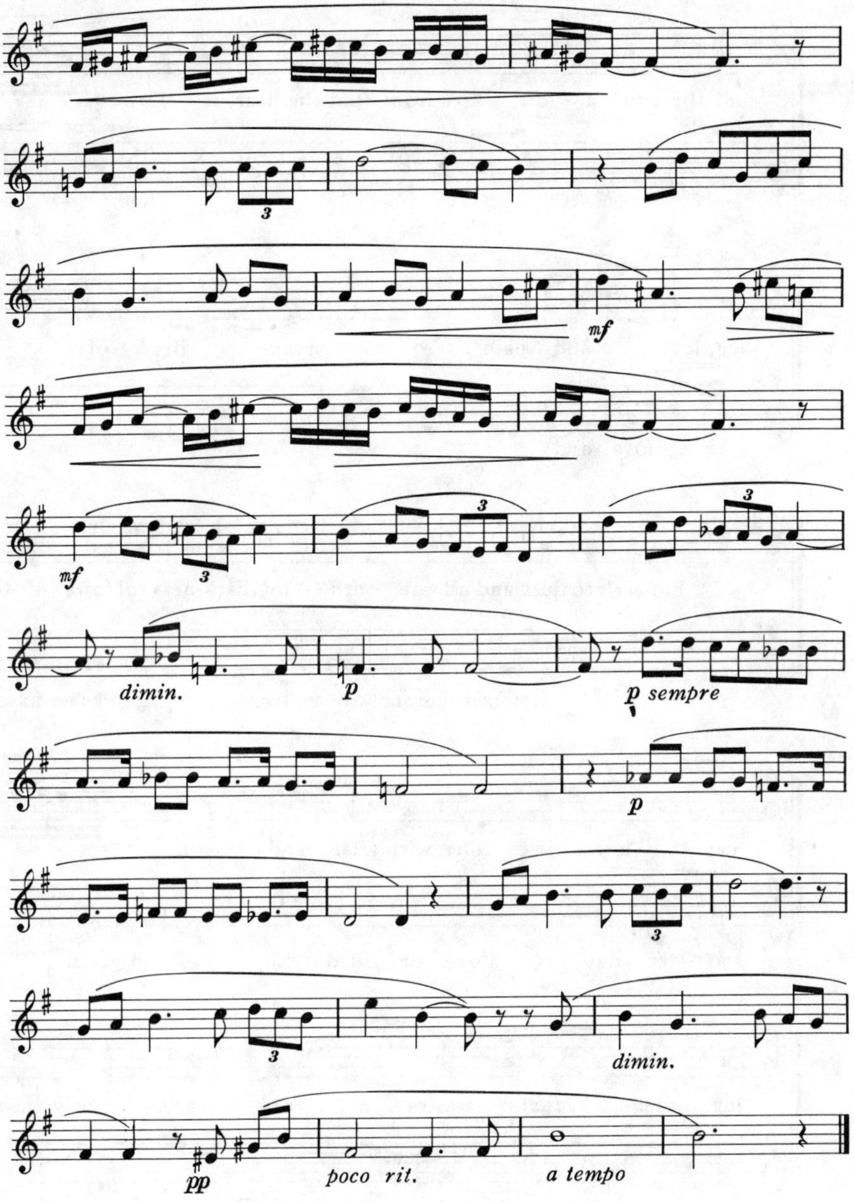
mf
mf
dimin.
p
p sempre
p
dimin.
pp
poco rit.
a tempo

Andante

Brahms, *Klänge*, Op. 66, No. 1

1060

p
From the earth the flow'rs are grow - ing, light from
p

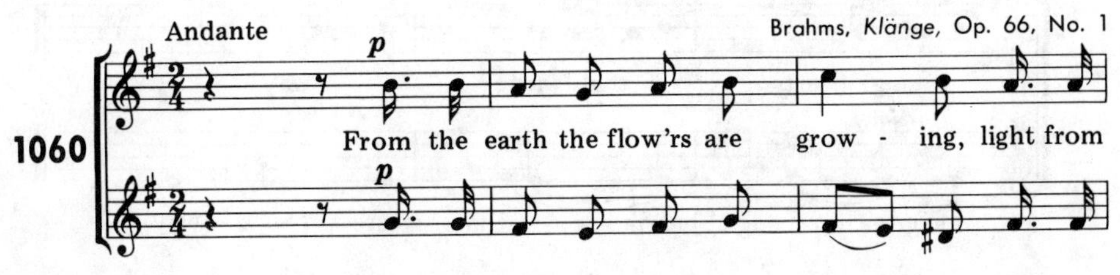

f
out the sun a - loft,. love from out the heart is flow - -
f
flow - -
ing, love and pain that breaks it oft.
ing, love and
p
Flower's to dust and ash are turn - ing, dark-ness fol-lows af - ter
p
Flow'rs to dust and ash are turn - ing dark-ness fol-lows
f
day, love is filled with grief and yearn - -
f
af - ter day, love is filled with grief and yearn - -
ing, grief that wastes sad hearts a-way, griev -
- - ing, grief that wastes sad hearts a-
dim.
- ing hearts that waste a-way.
dim.
way, griev - ing hearts that waste a - way.

1061

Allegro
mf
Handel, Semele
Each sa-cred min-strel tunes his lyre, and all in cho-rus.
join
and all
mf
in cho-rus join,
and all
in cho-rus
sa-cred min-strel tunes his lyre, and all in cho-rus join
join
and all,
and all in cho
-
rus
and all,
and all,
and all, in cho
-
rus
join.
Each sa-cred min-strel
join.
Each sa-cred min-strel tunes his lyre, and all in cho-rus
tunes his lyre, and all in cho-rus
join,
and all,
join,
and all,
and all,

and all
and all, in cho-rus join, and
in cho-rus join and all, and all, in cho-rus
all in cho-rus join Each sa-cred min-strel tunes his lyre, and
join and all, and all in
all in cho-rus join and all in
cho - rus join, in cho-rus join, and all,
cho - rus join, in cho-rus join,
and all in cho-rus join
and all and all and all
Adagio
and all, and all, in
and all, and all, in

cho - rus join, in cho - rus join.
cho - rus join, in cho - rus join.

CHAPTER 21

TWENTIETH CENTURY MELODY

Those composers of the twentieth century who strive to achieve originality by avoiding the primary characteristics of music of previous centuries do so in part through new concepts of meter and melody.

1. Meter. The meter in music is no longer bound to a system of regular recurring accents and an equal number of beats in the measure. The location of accented notes, and the length of the rhythmic groups these accents introduce, can vary up to the limit of the composer's imagination. Changing meter signatures, as seen in Chapter 17, are very common, but the use of these, or even constant measure lengths with a single meter signature, do not necessarily imply relatively weak and strong beats within the measure. Bar lines in these cases often function simply as a guide to the eye, recalling sixteenth century practice (review *Elementary Harmony, Theory and Practice,* pp. 139–42, "Another Metrical Concept").

2. Melody. The intervallic structure of the melodic line is often no longer influenced by an implied harmonic background. Without this implication, many individual melodic lines extracted from a composition often have little or no apparent meaning other than as a series of intervals. The musical effect of such a line is obvious only in the context of its setting with the other voices. Thus, singing such lines out of context depends upon instant recognition and performance of each melodic interval.

The preparatory exercises following have been chosen for drill in these two aspects of twentieth century composition.

Section 1. Rhythmic reading exercises.

Carter
1067
Messiaen
1068
*no meter signature
Copland
1069
Berg
1070

Section 2. Singing non-tonal lines.

Tone rows can be helpful as practice in singing an "abstract" series of intervals.[1] The *tone row* is a series of twelve tones, one each of the chromatic scale in any selected order. Since each tone is of equal importance, no impression of tonic or keynote is possible.

The tone rows which follow are derived from compositions of twentieth century composers. Each is in four forms:

P = Prime

I = Inversion (each interval of "P" moves the same distance but in the opposite direction)

R = Retrograde (the "P" row read from right to left)

RI = Retrograde Inversion

[1]See the author's *Advanced Harmony, Theory and Practice,* pages 371*ff* for more information on twelve-tone composition.

In creating a row and its derivations, any note may be in any octave; so, for example, the inversion of a major third up could be a minor sixth up (C up to E, inversion C down to A♭ or C up to A♭). Also, any note of the row may be spelled in any enharmonic version, since sharps and flats do not indicate melodic resolution tendencies (D♭ up to F, D♭ up to E♯, C♯ up to E♯, and C♯ up to F spell equally well this interval of four half steps).

Perform each row by thinking each interval carefully before singing. After singing "P," sing the "I" version by singing the last note of "P" and proceeding to the left on the staff. Do the same with "R" and "RI."

For additional practice, make up your own rows: (1) deliberately choose the order of tones, or (2) choose at random (for example, mark twelve cards, each with one pitch name; select one at a time, writing it on the staff until the row is complete). After writing the row, write out the other three versions.

1077
P→
←R
I→
←RI

1078
P→
←R
I→
←RI

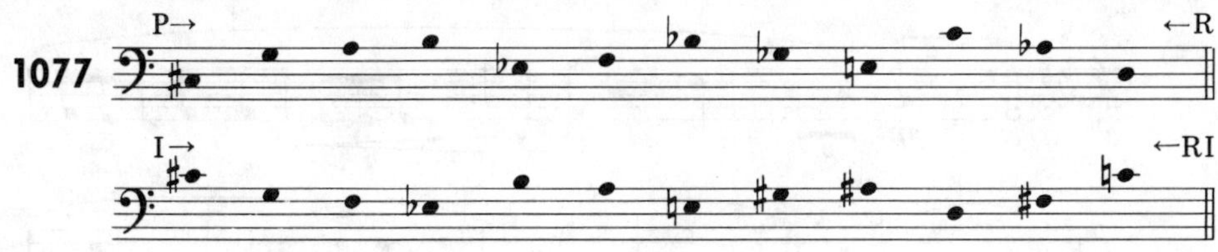

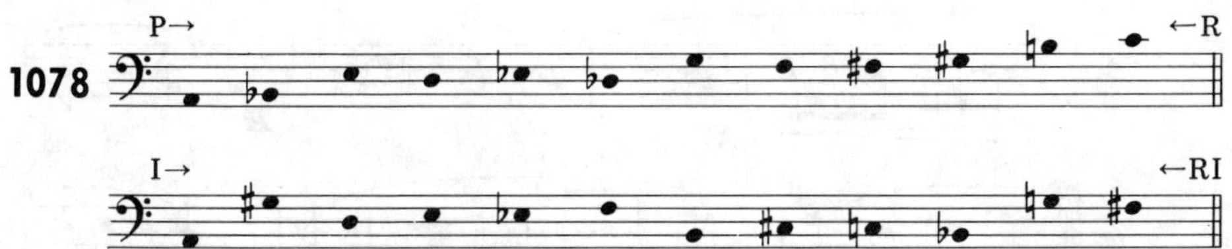

Section 3. Twentieth century melodies.

This group of melodies represents a selection from the many diverse styles to be found in the literature of the present century.

Debussy, *Mandoline*

1079
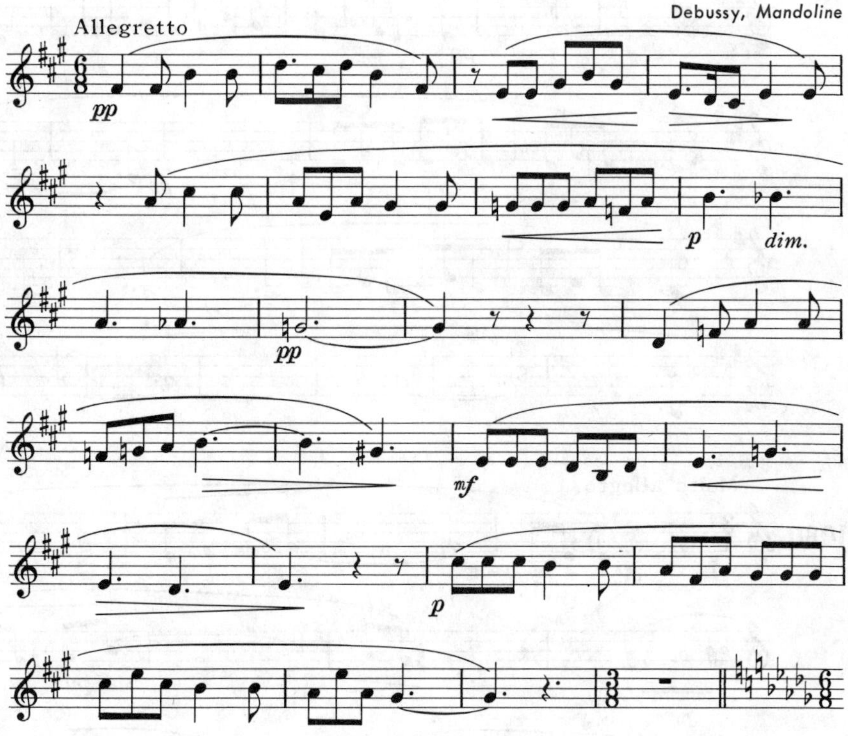
Allegretto
pp
p
dim.
pp
mf
p

pp
p
pp
più p
pp
pp
Molto allegro
R. Strauss, Elektra
1080
pp
sf
pp
sf
p
fp

Flowing — Hindemith, *Das Marienleben*, Op. 27

1081

mf p mf 2 mf p 2 2 2 poco f 2 p 2 2 pp 2 2 mf

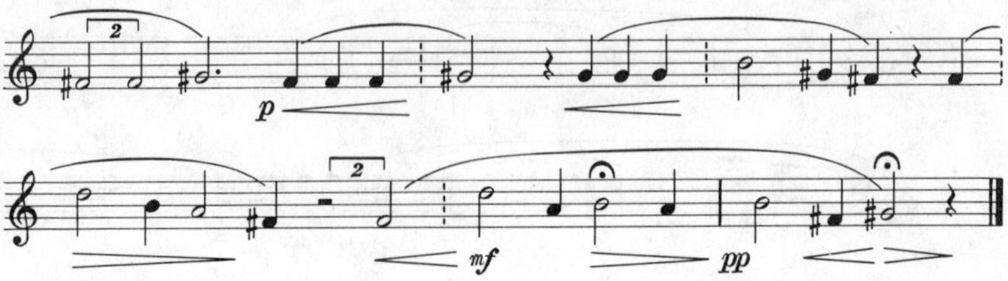

De Falla, *El Retablo de Maese Pedro*

Allegro semplicemente

1082

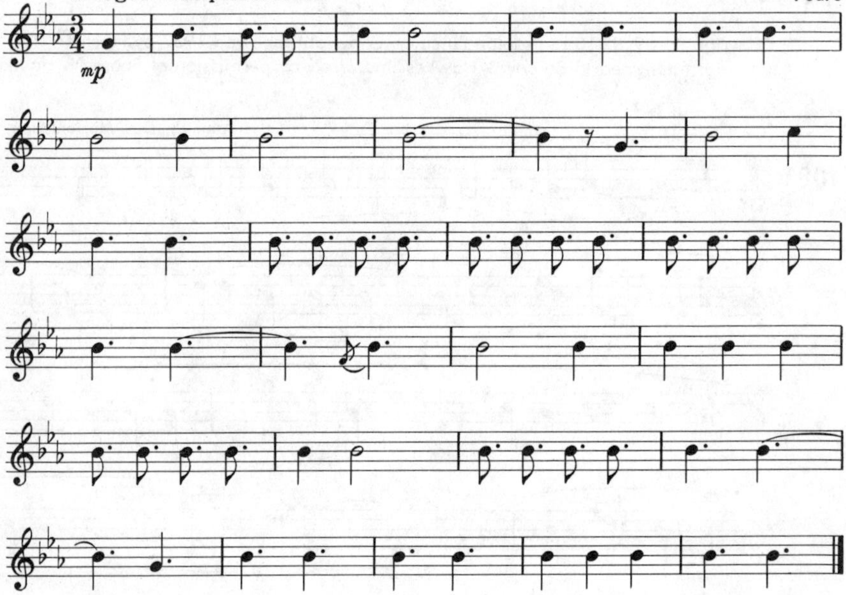

Ravel, *Les grands vents venus d'outremer*

Très agité

1083

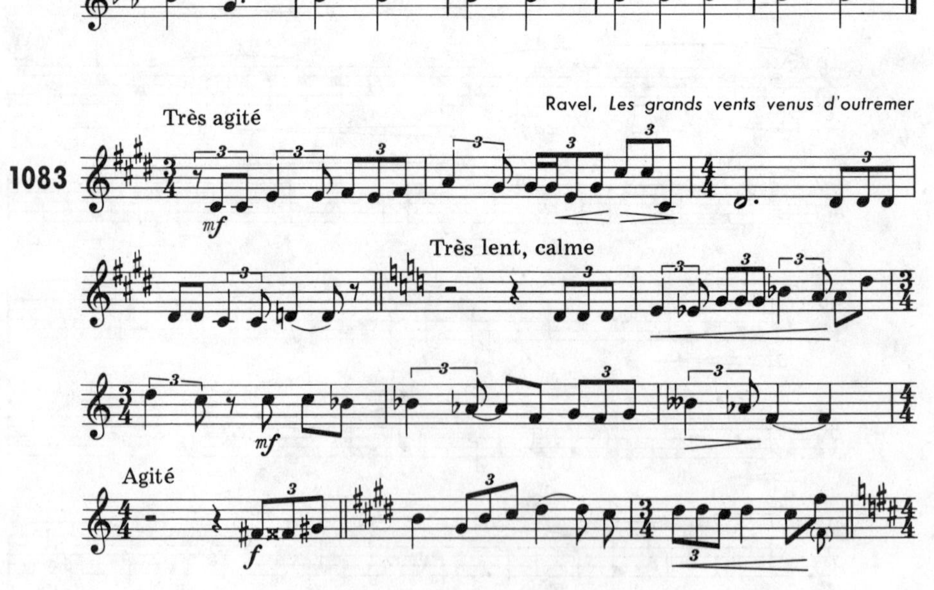

Walton, *Troilus and Cressida*

1084

* May sing an octave lower from this point.

From *Troilus and Cressida* by William Walton (1954). By permission of Oxford University Press.

Milhaud, *Vocalise-Étude*

1085

sans lenteur

p *très expressif*

p

mp

mf

p

pp

cédez - - - - - -

Copland, *Twelve Poems of Emily Dickinson*, "The Chariot"

1086

Prokofiev, *The Voice of Birds*, Op. 36, No. 2

1087

Schöenberg, *Schenk mir deinen goldenen Kamm*, Op. 2, No. 2 (1900)

1088

Etwas langsam

Schoenberg, *Tot*, Op. 48, No. 2 (1933)*

1089

* Two 12-tone rows are presented. How are they related? How do the last 4 measures relate to the row?

Allegro moderato

Ives, *Incantation*

1090

Scherzando

Stravinsky, *Renard*

1091

Section 4. Duets.

Merrill Ellis, Quintet for Oboe and Strings

1092

Allegro

Violin I

mf

Oboe

Vln. II

Vln. I

mp

sf

mp

sf

sfz

Stravinsky, *The Rake's Progress*

1093

♩.=132

THE RAKE'S PROGRESS (Music by Igor Stravinsky, Libretto by W.H. Auden and Chester Kallman) ©1949, 1950, 1951 by Boosey & Hawkes, Inc.; Renewed 1976, 1977, 1979. Reprinted by permission.

* In the composer's score, the part for harp is a series of block chords. Given here is the lowest note of each chord. transposed up one octave, with added figured bass symbols to indicate chord spellings. Play the complete harmony on the piano while singing the melody.

Shostakovich, Fugue No. 15, Op. 87

1095 Allegro molto

"24 PRELUDES AND FUGUES — Op.87" By DIMITRI SHOSTAKOVICH. Edited by Julien Musafia.

Bartók, Quartet No. 4

1096

CHAPTER 22

FOREIGN WORDS AND MUSICAL TERMS

This list contains only those foreign words used in this text. All words are Italian except as indicated: F = French; G = German.

a, à (F) by, at
al to the
accentuato accentuate
adagio slow, leisurely
agité (F) agitated
agitato agitated
al to
alla to the, at the, in the, in the style of
allant (F) stirring
allargando growing broader, slowing down with fuller tone (abbr. *allarg.*)
allegro lively, fast
andante moderately slow
andantino slower than andante
anima spirit
animando with growing animation
animé (F) animated
appassionato with passion
assai very

ben well
bien (F) well, very
brio vivacity, spirit, fire

calando decreasing loudness and slower tempo
calme (F) calm
cantabile in a singing style
commodo comfortable tempo
con with
crescendo increasing in volume (abbr. *cresc.*)

da capo from the beginning (abbr. *D.C.*)
dal segno from the sign (abbr. *D.S.*)
diminuendo decreasing in volume (abbr. *dim.*)
dolce soft
doloroso with pain or grief

espressivo expressively
et (F) and
etwas (G) somewhat

fine end
frisch (G) brisk, lively

gai (F) gay, brisk
giocoso playful
gracieusement (F) graciously
gracieux (F) gracious
grave slow, ponderous
grazia grace, elegance
grazioso graceful

heimlich (G) mysterious

im (G) in
innig (G) heartfelt, fervent
innigkeit (G) deep emotion

joyeux (F) joyous

ländler (G) a slow waltz-like dance
langsam (G) slow
larghetto not as slow as largo
largo slow and broad, stately
lebhaft (G) lively, animated
lent (F) slow
lenteur (F) slowness
lento slow
lentement (F) slowly

ma but
maestoso with majesty or dignity
marcato marked, emphatic
marcia march
mässig (G) moderate
mesto sad
mit (G) with
moderato moderately
modéré (F) moderately
molto much, very
mosso "moved"; *meno mosso* less rapid; *più mosso* more rapid
moto motion
munter (G) lively, animated

nicht (G) not
non not

pas (F) not
piano soft (abbr. *p*)
più more
poco little
presto very fast, rapid

rallentando slowing down (abbr. *rall.*)
rasch (G) quick
risoluto with resolution
ritardando slowing down (abbr. *rit.*)
ruhig (G) quiet

scherzando playfully
sans (F) without
schnell (G) fast
sehr (G) very
sempre always
sostenuto sustained
spirito spirit
spiritoso with spirit
stark (G) strong
subito suddenly

tempo giusto correct tempo
teneramente tenderly
très (F) very
triste (F) sad
tristement (F) sadly
trop (F) too much
troppo too much

volante light, swift
vif (F) lively
vite (F) quick
vivace very fast
vivo lively

zart (G) tender, delicate
ziemlich (G) somewhat, rather